D1473957

WALTER PATER: HUMANIST

WALTER PATER:
HUMANIST

Richmond Crinkley

The University Press of Kentucky

CONTENTS

"The human body in its beauty, as the highest potency of the beauty of material objects, seemed to him just then to be matter no longer, but, having taken celestial fire, to assert itself as indeed the true, though visible, soul or spirit in things."

"From that maxim of *Life as the end of life,* followed, as a practical consequence, the desirableness of refining all the instruments of inward and outward intuition, of developing all their capacities, of testing and exercising one's self in them, till one's whole nature became one complex medium of reception, towards the vision—the 'beatific vision,' if we really cared to make it such—of our actual experience in the world."

"It seemed just then as if the desire of the artist in him—that old longing to produce—might be satisfied by the exact and literal transcript of what was then passing around him, in simple prose, arresting the desirable moment as it passed, and prolonging its life a little.—To live in the concrete! To be sure, at least, of one's hold upon that!—Again, his philosophic scheme was but the reflection of the data of sense, and chiefly of sight, a reduction to the abstract, of the brilliant road he travelled on, through the sunlight"

MARIUS THE EPICUREAN

Preface

Walter Pater deserves better than he has received. Although his critical position has not been an enviable one in the first half of the twentieth century, he has never failed to be a point of reference for artists themselves—for Joyce and Yeats, in particular. And his impact on critical thinking has been a powerful one. The art criticism of Kenneth Clark is an example.

One of the reasons for Pater's eclipse is his style. To New Critics who demanded precision and to neo-Christians who demanded commitment, Pater seemed most unsatisfactory. He evades decision and casts his philosophical net wide. His points emerge, not from the epigrams of his disciple Wilde, but from complex and elaborately balanced paragraphs, skillfully built up from carefully selected example and modulated repetition.

The present study does not attempt to set a precise critical valuation upon Pater's work, but it does try to see some of his individual works in the context of his whole achievement and to suggest some of the complex ideas which Pater tries to realize through his prose— his understanding of "modernity" and relativism; his philosophy of art as a defence against the transiency of life and as a vehicle for the preservation and trans-mission of the human image; his vision of a many-sided life centered around the highest product of its culture, often the cathedral; and the moulding of his thought into fictional form, *Marius the Epicurean,* his finest achievement.

Preface

This volume began as a doctoral dissertation. I have worked on it for two years since it served its original purpose and hope I have purged it of some of the stylistic and structural deficiencies of the genre. Since, as noted above, Pater conveys his meaning in paragraphs and not in sentences, I have quoted liberally, trying to give enough of relevant passages to suggest the context.

I owe most thanks to Robert Langbaum, who patiently saw this work through its days as a dissertation, and to John Sparrow, who has made many helpful suggestions about it during later transmogrifications. Neither, needless to say, is at all responsible for its failings. I am also grateful to the United States-United Kingdom Educational Commission for a Fulbright fellowship, enabling me to live in Oxford and complete my work. Others to whom I owe warm thanks include Fredson Bowers, A. K. Davis, Jr., and Russell Hart at the University of Virginia; John Pope-Hennessy and Samuel Wright, both of whom made helpful suggestions regarding materials; Hugh Kenner, whose critical suggestions were helpful at an early stage in the work; Nicky Mariano, who took time to talk to me about Pater's influence on Bernard Berenson; and Megan Lloyd and Jean Baxter, who made valuable suggestions about annotation. And if I omit naming the many friends and family who have assisted with typing, proofreading, and other tasks, I trust they will know who they are and forgive me.

CHAPTER ONE

The Renaissance

To the modern spirit nothing is, or can
be rightly known except relatively under
conditions.

> Pater, "Coleridge's Writings"

Y EATS'S SELECTION AS the first modern poem of Walter Pater's passage describing the *Mona Lisa* has far-reaching esthetic implications.[1] Yeats notes that the *Mona Lisa* in her assimilated experience foreshadows "a philosophy, where the individual is nothing, the flux of *The Cantos* of Ezra Pound, objects without contour as in *Le Chef-d'oeuvre Inconnu,* human experience no longer shut into brief lives, cut off into this place and that place. . . ."[2]

Pound, Eliot, Joyce, Faulkner—each assimilates experience beyond the individual identity. The human figure in art, transcending its individuality, becomes for them an image summing up a full range of historical experience. The time scheme of modern literature defined by Yeats in his introduction echoes Pater's *Mona Lisa* passage: "Time cannot be divided." All events become as one for modern man, as they are for Pater's La Gioconda.

Yeats recognizes the symbolic nature of the *Mona Lisa* in Pater's description. The painting as Pater describes it synthesizes classical and Christian elements, conveying strong suggestions of meaning not easily defined. The musical analogy in the passage—La Gioconda's experience is "but the sound of lyres and flutes"—evokes the suggestiveness of the painting and effectively denies the possibility of any specific philosophical content. In Pater's description, the painting presents itself as an example of the modern and it has no explicit "meaning." "Lady Lisa" as symbol represents the modern because she combines in herself the intellectual forces for which Pater values the Renaissance. Her assimilation of these forces and the reader's response to them exemplify in microcosm the theme of *Studies in the History of the Renaissance,* Pater's first important collection of essays and still his most famous book.[3]

Reader's often accept Pater's injunction "to know one's own impression of the object of art as it really is, to discriminate it, to realise it distinctly" as the principal message of the "Preface" to *The Renaissance.*[4] But they sometimes pay insufficient attention to the succeeding explanation of the uniqueness of the individual impression, which is far more essential to an understanding of the volume's structure and Pater's critical purpose. The individual impression is important to Pater because the greatest works of art are so varied in their content and appeal that no one response will suffice. Each individual brings his own experience, his own criteria, to the work of art—even though, as Yeats says, the individual has ceased to be important as a subject for art. But the work of art, by its very variety, justifies the highly individual (or relativistic) approach.

> The objects with which aesthetic criticism deals— music, poetry, artistic and accomplished forms of human life—are indeed receptacles of so many powers or forces; they possess, like the products of nature, so many virtues or qualities. What is this song or picture, this engaging personality presented in life or in a book, to *me?*[5]

In the second half of the twentieth century, Pater's insistence on the necessity of the unique individual experience of art would seem a trite and obvious criterion of esthetic judgment. One reason Pater's position seems so obvious, however, is that he did such a good job of proselytizing for it. Through Wilde's inversion of the usual clichés about the relationship of art to life, through Yeats's insistence on a recondite and highly artificial stance by the artist himself, and through Joyce's epiphanies, Pater's viewpoint has come to be the common one. Not that Pater was alone in holding this view of the relationship of the apprehender and the work of art. Goethe, Gautier, and the Pre-Raphaelites come to mind, all of whom either influenced Pater or expressed similar esthetic standards independently. But Pater stands as the consistent and consecrated prophet of the egocentric approach to art. His whole body of critical and creative work devotes itself to trying to find how the individual, so restricted by his own peculiar limitations of perception, can use and understand and identify with the vast and multifaceted body of creative work, and, indeed, of experience, around him.

The structure of *The Renaissance* has a certain inner logic: the volume begins and ends with a focus on the apprehender. The "Preface," at least initially, and the "Conclusion" instruct the individual on his uses of art (that is, the materials presented in the essays) and on the rewards he may expect from it. The essays themselves stand as Pater's body of impressions gathered from the works of a particular period. The intense sensuousness of Pater's impressions may indicate his reaction to Ruskin. Sir Kenneth Clark notes that whereas Ruskin, as if in reaction, asserts a rigidly moralistic view of art, Pater virtually ignores any specific moral application of the works with which he deals.[6] Even what Pater calls the "higher morality" consists more of a willing acceptance of both art and experience than of a mode of behavior.[7] Pater in the Wordsworth essay emphasizes means; Ruskin emphasizes ends. Pater's reader may use

5

the data presented as he will, for "one must realise such primary data for one's self, or not at all."[8] Yet what Pater calls the esthetic critic—or what we now call the impressionistic critic—deals with data of a particular kind. A description of the kinds of data and an analysis of various examples provide the subject matter for the main essays of *The Renaissance*.

Pater makes quite clear in the "Preface" the intended catholicity of his approach to art. The materials with which the critic works should not be of any one period or school; "[For the critic] all periods, types, schools of taste, are in themselves equal."[9] Here, as elsewhere, Pater uses the word receptacle to describe the work of art. The implications of the usage do not become clear until the argument has proceeded. He describes the Renaissance as a "complex, many-sided" movement.[10] One of the changes that characterize history, in Pater's philosophy of culture, is a movement from dogmatic belief in one philosophical system or set of values to a relativistic acceptance or tolerance of a variety of philosophical systems or sets of values. The reverse change—from relativism to dogma—also takes place. The Renaissance, like the modern age, Pater's own time, is characterized by relativism. In its Italian manifestation, not only the concrete works of art but the "general spirit and character" and the "ethical qualities of which it is a consummate type" make the Renaissance worthy of the critic's attention. "The fifteenth century in Italy is one of these happier eras. . . . it is an era productive in personalities, many-sided, centralised, complete."[11] The complexity of spirit communicates itself to the artist and "gives unity to all the various products of the Renaissance."[12] The work of art is a receptacle in that it takes into itself and assimilates the complexity of its age and assumes new complexities as it passes through history. The *Mona Lisa* is the prime example. Yeats recognizes the same characteristics as Pater in much Renaissance art. The fullness and complexity of experience stand as dominant characteristics of these works of art— or at least as dominant characteristics of these works of art as we see them. Yeats puts it well in his essay "The Holy Mountain":

> Does not every civilisation as it approaches or recedes from its full moon seem as it were to shiver into the premonition of some perfection born out of itself, perhaps even of some return to its first Source? Does not one discover in the faces of Madonnas and holy women painted by Raphael or da Vinci, if never before or since, a condition of soul where all is still and finished, all experience wound up upon a bobbin? Does one not hear those lips murmur that, despite whatever illusion we cherish, we came from no immaturity, but out of our own perfection like ships that "all their swelling canvas wear"? Does not every new civilisation, upon the other hand, imagine that it was born in revelation, or that it comes from dependence upon dark or unknown powers, that it can but open its eyes with difficulty after some long night's sleep or winter's hibernation?[13]

Yeats's argument addresses itself to a variety of points. Central to an understanding of Pater's relativism, however, is his description of the work of art (especially the Renaissance work of art) as a summary of experience, a realization of the complexity out of which it was born and through which it has passed. Individual experience, represented by the work of art, becomes cultural ex-

7

perience, which in turn influences individual experience, finally represented by the apprehender. Equilibrium and motion coexist in the *Mona Lisa.*

Pater's essay on Coleridge (1866) is probably the best of his literary essays and the most clearly worded explanation of his cultural relativism. The essay on Winckelmann, the longest in *The Renaissance* and the first of that series of essays to be published, appeared only a year later. Four of the other essays appeared in the *Fortnightly Review,* and *The Renaissance* itself in 1873. The philosophical connections between the essays of *The Renaissance* and "Coleridge's Writings" are important, and the Coleridge essay has a particular relevance to Pater's interpretation of the Renaissance as a historical period. Not only the relativistic approach to experience of the "Conclusion" but also the cultural relativism of the "Preface" and the other essays in *The Renaissance* find their germinal expression in the 1866 essay on Coleridge.

"Coleridge's Writings" appeared in the *Westminster Review.*[14] Although the essay itself gained no immediate reputation for its author, it marked an impressive beginning for the young critic. It remains not only a good interpretation of Coleridge—seeing him as a seeker of absolutes in a relativistic age—but also the most valuable introduction to Pater's thought. Unlike Coleridge, Pater welcomes the relativism he understands as characteristic of his time. Pater's definition of relativism must be understood clearly at the outset, for his use of the term is markedly precise and dependent on information not always available in the immediate context of any single essay.

 Certain historical periods—such as the Renaissance, the Greece of Plato, and the modern age—exhibit a cultural complexity which Pater defines as relativism. For Pater, cultural complexity means the availability of a number of philosophical positions and modes of esthetic expression. The adherents of any one system of thought may recognize several valid alternatives to their own system. Aurelian Rome, for example, appears in *Marius the Epicurean* as a period in which the sensitive individual has a fuller access to the train of experience and the comprehensive body of art and thought than he does in a more dogmatic age, such as the Reformation. To Pater, the modern age seems to be the most complete historical realization of the relativistic spirit: the relativistic periods in history before the modern anticipate it and in the modern age we see the culmination, the seemingly full and permanent fruition, of relativistic thought. "Modern thought," asserts Pater in the essay on Coleridge,

> is distinguished from ancient by its cultivation of the 'relative' spirit in place of the 'absolute.' Ancient philosophy sought to arrest every object in an eternal outline, to fix thought in a necessary formula, and types of life in a classification by 'kinds' or *genera*. To the modern spirit nothing is, or can be rightly known except relatively under conditions.[15]

The "eternal outline" in which ancient philosophy sought to fix thought gives way to the "receptacle" of the "Preface" to *The Renaissance*. It might be said that the "Preface" modifies the essay on Coleridge in one important respect. Although ancient philosophy fails to fix "every object in an eternal outline," surely classic art does give us objects in eternal outlines; but the implications of the object, the responses which it

9

evokes, are in constant flux. As Pater states in the "Preface," providing a convenient link with the Coleridge essay, "Beauty, like all other qualities presented to human experience, is relative; and the definition of it becomes unmeaning and useless in proportion to its abstractness." Pater rejects any abstract theory of beauty and prefers the practical test of the individual's response to the object with which he is confronted.

For Pater the modern period demonstrates its relativism through the comprehensiveness of its sympathies. The origins of these comprehensive sympathies lie in the physical sciences, Pater implies:

> The moral world is ever in contact with the physical; the relative spirit has invaded moral philosophy from the ground of the inductive science. There it has started a new analysis of the relations of body and mind, good and evil, freedom and necessity. Hard and abstract moralities are yielding to a more exact estimate of the subtlety and complexity of our life.[16]

As already noted, Pater analyzes Coleridge's intellectual position as the continuing struggle of an absolutist in a relativistic age. Thus Coleridge's career becomes an effort to construct systems for a world more obviously than before involved in philosophical ferment, a ferment which resists systems. And Coleridge himself becomes the type of the absolutist, who, paradoxically, makes up part of the relativist's world.

> Coleridge, with his passion for the absolute, for something fixed where all is moving, his faintness, his broken memory, his intellectual disquiet, may still be ranked among the interpreters of one of the constituent elements of our life.[17]

10

As the representative of "the modern," Coleridge, "by what he did, what he was, and what he failed to do, represents that inexhaustible discontent, languor, and homesickness, the chords of which ring all through our modern literature."[18] The problem pervades Pater's writings, and he solves it in various ways.

Although Pater's evaluation of his own "modern" age derives to some extent from Darwin and from developments in the physical sciences (and doubtless from the theological debates occasioned by Darwin's writings) there are equally obvious sources not at all related to the physical sciences.[19] It can hardly be doubted, for example, that Mill's *On Liberty*, with its doctrine that some part of truth might be found in even the most despised opinion, influenced the impressionable Pater. And then there is Matthew Arnold, with whom T. S. Eliot so rightly ties Pater.[20]

Eliot's aim is to denigrate Arnold. He notes that "only when religion has been partly retired and confined, when an Arnold can sternly remind us that Culture is wider than Religion, do we get 'religious art' and in due course 'aesthetic religion.' "[21] Eliot sought to discredit Arnold by making him responsible for Pater and Pater's estheticism, but he might well have made a more direct criticism of Arnold.

When Pater came to Queen's College, Oxford, in 1858, Arnold had been Professor of Poetry for only a short time. (He was appointed in 1857.) Thomas Wright, Pater's erratic biographer, tells us that Pater went to hear a number of Arnold's lectures and that it was Arnold's influence that led to Pater's reverence for Goethe and Sénancour.[22] Wright's specific assertions, for which there is only the most meagre documentation, might be questioned, but given that an eminent and articulate Arnold and a curious and literarily-inclined Pater were lecturer and student at Oxford at the same time, the influence would seem obvious and inescapable.

Arnold's inaugural lecture as Professor of Poetry was not, as Arnold states in a prefatory note to it, printed at the time he gave it.[23] The lecture was delivered before Pater came to Oxford, but "there appeared at the time several comments on it from critics who had either heard it, or heard reports about it."[24] Arnold goes on to say that "[the lecture] was meant to be followed and completed by a course of lectures developing the subject entirely, and some of these were given." The ideas of the inaugural lecture, "On the Modern Element in Literature," then, were much discussed and even written about, and Arnold himself developed them in further lectures. His principal ideas must have been known as much to Pater as to any other undergraduate.

There are several points of conjunction of Pater's thought, as outlined in the Coleridge essay, with Arnold's. It would almost be fair, in fact, to say that much of Pater's philosophy of culture is implicit in Arnold's lecture. Arnold defines modernity much as Pater does:

> A significant, a highly-developed, a culminating epoch, on the one hand,—a comprehensive, a commensurate, an adequate literature, on the other,— these will naturally be the objects of deepest interest to our modern age. Such an epoch and such a literature are, in fact, *modern,* in the same sense in which our own age and literature are modern; they are founded upon a rich past and upon an instructive fulness of experience.[25]

Pater does not make the point that the complex age also must have a commensurate literature, but he does imply that Coleridge's writings are particularly fitting for his times, given the character of Coleridge. Indeed, Arnold seems to give us a précis of Pater's interpretation of Coleridge in his lecture:

> The predominance of thought, of reflection, in modern epochs is not without its penalties; in the unsound, in the overtasked, in the over-sensitive, it has produced the most painful, the most lamentable results; it has produced a state of feeling unknown to less enlightened but perhaps healthier epochs—the feeling of depression, the feeling of *ennui*.[26]

Surely here is "that inexhaustible discontent, languor, and homesickness" which Pater sees in Coleridge and which was to inhabit his own writing. Arnold identified the type and Pater made a specific critical application.

Like Pater's, Arnold's "modern" periods are many. Arnold, for example, compares Periclean Athens to Elizabethan England to see what characteristics the two periods have in common, characteristics which might be called modern. He identifies six: (1) men move securely "within the limits of civil life"; (2) "an enlarged knowledge" leads to "the growth of a tolerant spirit"—"a spirit patient of the diversities of habits and opinions"; (3) "the multiplication of the conveniences of life"; (4) "the formation of taste"; (5) "the capacity for refined pursuits"; and (6) "the supreme characteristic of all: the intellectual maturity of man himself; the tendency to observe facts with a critical spirit; to search for their law, not to wander among them at random; to judge by the rule of reason, not by the impulse of prejudice or caprice."[27]

Of these characteristics, Pater most readily takes hold of the second, like Arnold, however, implicitly acknowledging its dependence on the first. Civil order provides the basis for a tolerant society, and it may even extend to international limits at times, making the relations between nations more capable of disinterest. Arnold quotes Pericles as saying, "We have freedom for individual diversities of opinions and character; we do not take offence at the tastes and habits of our neighbour if they differ from our own."[28] In Arnold the young Pater found an authoritative critic whose cultural relativism sanctioned his own. It was always with Arnold's ideas in the background that Pater applied himself to the essays that make up *The Renaissance*.

In *The Renaissance,* relativism involves the perception of a broadly defined and variegated culture. The resolution of the problems presented by the culture lies in the individual's accustoming himself to the perceptive act, which at its highest point of concentration becomes an arresting of the flux by its very intensity—the "hard, gemlike flame" manifesting itself as the ideal in human experience. Memory is evoked and the "faculty for truth is a power of distinguishing and fixing delicate and fugitive details."[29]

Pater interprets the Renaissance as a period of relativistic synthesis. Like other periods of relativism, the Renaissance will give way to an age of dogma—specifically to the dogma of the Reformation. The culture of the Renaissance comprehends varied and even seemingly conflicting modes of thought and expression. And the Renaissance resembles nineteenth-century Europe in its relativism, as Pater notes in his introduction to C. L. Shadwell's edition of Dante:

> A minute sense of the external world and its beauties, a minute sense of the phenomena of the mind, of what is beautiful and of interest there, a demand for wide and cheering outlooks on religion, for a largeness of spirit in its application to life:—these are the special points of contact between Dante and the genius of our own century.[30]

Dante and Coleridge serve as examples of great minds dealing with two historical manifestations of an increasing liberality of spirit that Pater calls "relativism." As critic, Pater describes the nature of the relativistic synthesis and enumerates its individual manifestations in art and literature. By assuming the role of critical delineator of a cultural synthesis, Pater can set exceptionally comprehensive limits for his period. The definition of Renaissance offered in the "Preface" and the essays enables Pater to assemble a broad range of data that illustrate his philosophy of culture. The comely receptacle have an impact beyond their specifically historical contexts.

Pater gives one of his best definitions of Renaissance at the beginning of "Two Early French Stories":

> The word *Renaissance,* indeed, is now generally used to denote not merely the revival of classical antiquity which took place in the fifteenth century, and to which the word was first applied, but a whole complex movement, of which that revival of classical antiquity was but one element or symptom. For us the *Renaissance* is the name of a

many-sided but yet united movement, in which the love of the things of the intellect and the imagination for their own sake, the desire for a more liberal and comely way of conceiving life, make themselves felt, urging those who experience this desire to search out first one and then another means of intellectual or imaginative enjoyment, and directing them not only to the discovery of old and forgotten sources of this enjoyment, but to the divination of fresh sources thereof—new experiences, new subjects of poetry, new forms of art.[31]

With this definition as background, Pater makes his assertion that the "rupture between the middle age and the Renaissance . . . has so often been exaggerated."[32] Yet the most pertinent fact is the comprehensiveness of spirit that allows the Renaissance in Pater's interpretation to encompass so much. He states explicitly in his review of Symonds's *The Italian Renaissance* what he means by "a more liberal and comely way of conceiving life":

The Renaissance is an assertion of liberty indeed, but of liberty to see and feel those things the seeing and feeling of which generate not the "barbarous ferocity of temper, the savage and coarse tastes" of the Renaissance Popes, but a sympathy with life everywhere, even in its weakest and most frail manifestations.[33]

Sympathetic and sensuous response dominate Pater's cultural definitions as they do his fictions; indeed, Pater seems to suggest that "seeing and feeling"—sensuous response—is more conducive to sympathy than is withdrawal or narrowness, which may lead to "barbarous ferocity of temper."

The Renaissance

The definition of the Renaissance at the beginning of "Two Early French Stories," like that in the review of Symonds's book, is expansionist and liberal. Pater indicates in both that intellect in the period he writes about builds on its own strength rather than on a dogmatic system presented to it. The classical revival, in a set of alternatives familiar to Pater's style, may be an element or a symptom of the "complex movement." It is probably both, a symptom because complexity expresses itself in seeking after self-identifying equivalents, and an element because the classical revival exists as a primary constituent part of the humanism of the Renaissance. The Greeks' interest in the things of this world (and the imprecisely defined and sometimes seemingly proto-Christian "sweetness") enters the Christian era in the Renaissance, and the Renaissance has no existence without this Greek element.

The expansion of intellect and feeling—or the "assertion of liberty"—of the Renaissance expresses itself through Abelard:

> In this uncertain twilight . . . his relation to the general beliefs of his age has always remained. In this, as in other things, he prefigures the character of the Renaissance, that movement in which, in various ways, the human mind wins for itself a new kingdom of feeling and sensation and thought, not opposed to but only beyond and independent of the spiritual system then actually realised. The opposition into which Abelard is thrown, which gives its colour to his career, which breaks his soul to pieces, is a no less subtle opposition than that between the merely professional, official, hireling ministers of that system, with their ignorant worship of system for its own sake, and the true child

of light, the humanist, with reason and heart and senses quick, while theirs were almost dead. He reaches out towards, he attains, modes of ideal living, beyond the prescribed limits of that system, though in essential germ, it may be, contained within it.[34]

In his analysis of Abelard's character, Pater deals in concepts far larger than those of the merely historical individual. Or rather, he deals with an individual whose biography has broad cultural implications.

The medieval Abelard finds a place in Pater's scheme because he does not fit easily into any restrictive spiritual system. More pertinent to the large argument of *The Renaissance,* however, Abelard ventures intellectually beyond the approved interests of the medieval spiritual system. Thus he becomes the first humanist in *The Renaissance.* Abelard's intellectual expansionism fits well with the liberality of thought of the French Renaissance and anticipates the Italian Renaissance. Pater sees the movement from Romanesque to Gothic as a humanizing phenomenon; it signifies for him a stirring of the spirit that eventually links pagan and Christian.

Using the theme, derived from Heine, of the wandering of the old gods about the earth after their downfall, Pater notes that the venture beyond the Christian ideal involves a possible establishment of opposing poles of thought:

In their search after the pleasures of the senses and the imagination, in their care for beauty, in their worship of the body, people were impelled beyond the bounds of the Christian ideal; and their love became sometimes a strange idolatry, a strange rival religion. It was the return of that ancient Venus, not dead, but only hidden for a time in the caves of the Venusberg, of those old pagan gods still going to and fro on the earth under all sorts of disguises.[35]

Pater is careful, however, to point out that the "strange rival religion" is less rival than complement. The rival religion has bounds paradoxically broad enough to include the system to which it is opposed: "in the *House Beautiful* the saints, too, have their place."[36]

Wright asserts that Pater, at the time he was writing the essay on Coleridge, considered becoming a Unitarian minister.[37] The suggestion is plausible. Certainly Pater exhibits a kind of cultural unitarianism, akin to Arnold's, which takes comprehensiveness of intellectual sympathy and liberality of viewpoint as the highest virtues. These central characteristics distinguish the Renaissance from other periods in history and provide a safeguard against the charge that Pater might have found much the same things in any age:

> The student of the Renaissance has this advantage over the student of the emancipation of the human mind in the Reformation, or the French Revolution, that in tracing the footsteps of humanity to higher levels, he is not beset at every turn by the inflexibilities and antagonisms of some well-recognised controversy, with rigidly defined opposites, exhausting the intelligence and limiting one's sympathies. The opposition of the professional defenders of a mere system to that more sincere and generous play of the forces of human mind and character, which I have noted as the secret of Abelard's struggle, is, indeed always powerful. But the incompatibility with one another of souls really "fair" is not essential; and within the enchanted region of the Renaissance one needs not

19

be forever on one's guard. Here there are no fixed parties, no exclusions: all breathes of that unity of culture in which "whatsoever things are comely" are reconciled for the elevation and adorning of our spirits. And just in proportion as those who took part in the Renaissance become centrally representative of it, just so much the more is this condition realised in them.[38]

By recognizing that his definition is stipulative, Pater builds up a defence against critics who might take him to task historically: his subjects exemplify comprehensive intellectual sympathy only to the extent that they are representative of the Renaissance.

The contrast of the Renaissance with the Reformation and the French Revolution goes far to explain Pater's relativism. For him, cultural relativism, epitomized in the Renaissance, excludes only exclusiveness, and hence the sense of controversy and party characterizing the other two periods is alien to both his relativistic and his synthetic spirit. Thus Pater's Botticelli accepts the "middle world" of the angels who took no side in the Revolt of Lucifer, although Dante scorns them as "unworthy alike of heaven and hell."[39]

Abelard, Aucassin, Amis, and Amile exemplify the noncontentious and expansive culture of the Renaissance. Pater's emphasis falls on the secular virtues, such as love and friendship. Pico della Mirandola serves as the exemplar of the stylistic grace which draws the interest to forgotten lore. As a fifteenth-century scholar who attempts to make Greek religion compatible with Christianty, Pico appeals to Pater because he exhibits the same breadth of outlook found in Abelard. The large theme, as in "Two Early French Stories," is reconciliation. But Pico appeals more to the stylist in Pater: he makes comely and desirable the forgotten material

with which he deals—whether it be the Platonism received through Ficino or "the secrets of ancient philos-
ophies." Pater describes Pico's learning as "strange,
confused, uncritical"—somewhat the same description
Eliot gives sixty years later of Pater's erudition in
Marius:

> *Marius* itself is incoherent; its method is a number
> of fresh starts; its content is a hodge-podge of the
> learning of the classical don, the impressions of the
> sensitive holiday visitor to Italy, and a prolonged
> flirtation with the liturgy.[40]

What Eliot sees as a flaw, Pater sees as a virtue. It
makes little difference that Pico's sources may be less
than satisfactory.

> It is said that in his eagerness for mysterious learn-
> ing he once paid a great sum for a collection of
> cabalistic manuscripts, which turned out to be
> forgeries; and the story might well stand as a
> parable of all he ever seemed to gain in the way
> of actual knowledge.[41]

Pico's virtue is that he can assimilate gracefully.
The intrinsic value of the materials with which Pico
deals is much less important than his feeling that they
connect him with other men in other times, with modes
of thought previously unknown to him. His intent is
to seek renewal through finding some still vital element
in human experience that has been seemingly forgotten
or ignored.
According to Pater, Pico's reader enjoys the sensation
of discovery:

> To read a page of one of Pico's forgotten books is
> like a glance into one of those ancient sepulchres,

upon which the wanderer in classical lands has
sometimes stumbled, with the old disused ornaments and furniture of a world wholly unlike ours
still fresh in them.[42]

In this passage, perhaps more than anywhere else in
The Renaissance, we sense Pater's identification of himself with his subject. Although Pico's conception of
nature is "so different" from the modern, his use of his
materials resembles that of Pater. The continuing
interest in what has been lost characterizes the work
of both. The furniture and ornaments in the newly
discovered tomb are nothing more than Pater's re-
covered images—the literary medium, like the sepulchre,
preserves the creations of the human mind for the
diligent seeker of a later age.

Certainly Pater's solipsistic description of Pico's
"figured style" evokes the author of *The Renaissance*
as much as the author of the *Heptaplus.*[43] And the
Platonic passage made by Pico "from the love of a
physical object to the love of unseen beauty" resembles
the passage made by both Florian Deleal in "The Child
in the House" and the young Marius, the former being
avowedly autobiographical, the latter less so.[44] The
"Symposium" comes to mind as a primary source; with
Pater, however, the love of the unseen remains very
closely tied to the love of the visible.

Most significantly, Pico's artistic cultivation of the
modes of thought of the Renaissance corresponds to
Pater's own:

Of this artistic reconciliation [of the pagan and the
Christian by the painters of the period] work like
Pico's was but the feebler counterpart. Whatever
philosophers had to say on one side or the other,

whether they were successful or not in their attempts to reconcile the old to the new, and to justify the expenditure of so much care and thought on the dreams of a dead faith, the imagery of the Greek religion, the direct charm of its story, were by artists valued and cultivated for their own sake. Hence a new sort of mythology, with a tone and qualities of its own. . . . that mythology of the Italian Renaissance. . . . grew up from the mixture of two traditions, two sentiments, the sacred and the profane.[45]

This evaluation of Renaissance mythology represents the most explicit commentary in the essays themselves on the "Conclusion." It also gives us a view of Pico's art that works equally well for Pater's. Both Pico and Pater comprehend the artistic act, but the work of description and interpretation becomes a "feebler counterpart." And the counterpart embodies, like the works of art it describes, a "new mythology," comprehensive in its reconciliations and its assimilations.

Ezra Pound's description of Pater's appeal seems relevant when one reads Pater's interpretation of Pico. Pound writes that Pater is "adolescent reading" and "very excellent bait."[46] So, according to Pater himself, is Pico. "He will not let one go; he wins one in spite of one's self, to turn again to the pages of his forgotten books, although we know already that the actual solution proposed in them will satisfy us as little as perhaps it satisfied him."[47] Yet both Pater and Pico attempt their syntheses, Pico with his nine hundred paradoxes and Pater with his syntheses of the Greek, Roman, and Renaissance cultures. Both believe in the continued vitality of what has moved men before and both attempt to capture it in its fullness.

In *The Renaissance* Pater sees his function as critic or "appreciator" of culture as a dual one: he presents the culture to be apprehended and he also offers instruction on the means of apprehension. Just as the Coleridge essay stands as the initial explicit statement of Pater's philosophy of culture, the idealized portrait "Diaphaneitè," an incomplete sketch which Pater wrote in 1864 and read to Old Mortality, an Oxford society, offers a first and tentative sketch of the ideal apprehender.[48]

In "Diaphaneitè" Pater identifies, for the purposes of classifying esthetically-minded persons, two "unworldly types of character."[49] The first includes saints, artists, and speculative thinkers—in other words, the creators, "those who theorise about its [the world's] unsoundness." These makers have "a breadth and generality of character."[50] The alternative unworldly type is less clearly defined. Wright translates the term as "Crystal Man," and this translation of *diaphaneitè* seems to work as well as any.[51] The term fittingly describes an ideal of character that appears repeatedly in Pater's writings under various guises. The second type "crosses" the main current of life and serves as the transmitter of "the life quickened at single points."[52] The second type, then, interprets or redefines the work of the creators for other creators and presumably for other segments of humanity.

This second type has the additional virtue of being assimilative: "Sibi unitus et simplificatus esse."[53] From "Diaphaneitè," one begins to perceive what Pater means by "seeing things [works of art, persons] as they are":

> The spirit . . . is the very opposite of that which regards life as a game of skill, and values things

and persons as marks or counters of something to be gained, or achieved, beyond them. It seeks to value everything at its eternal worth, not adding to it, or taking from it, the amount of influence it may have for or against its own special scheme of life. It is the spirit that sees external circumstances as they are, its own power and tendencies as they are, and realises the given conditions of life, not disquieted by the desire for change, or the preference of one part of life rather than another, or passion, or opinion. The character we mean to indicate achieves this perfect life by a happy gift of nature, without any struggle at all.[54]

The passage goes on to note that both "unworldly" types, creator and transmitter, possess this spirit, although their practical aims exist for different purposes, perhaps on different levels.[55] Yeats's projection of his child's ideal personality in "A Prayer for My Daughter" makes the point:

> May she become a flourishing hidden tree
> That all her thoughts may like the linnet be,
> And have no business but dispensing round
> Their magnanimities of sound. . . .

And

> An intellectual hatred is the worst,
> So let her think opinions are accursed.
> Have I not seen the loveliest woman born
> Out of the mouth of Plenty's horn,
> Because of her opinionated mind
> Barter that horn and every good
> By quiet natures understood
> For an old bellows full of angry wind?

Considering that, all hatred driven hence,
The soul recovers radical innocence
And learns at last that it is self-delighting,
Self-appeasing, self-affrighting,
And that its own sweet will is Heaven's will;
She can, though every face should scowl
And every windy quarter howl
Or every bellows burst, be happy still.

And may her bridegroom bring her to a house
Where all's accustomed, ceremonious;
For arrogance and hatred are the wares
Peddled in the thoroughfares,
How but in custom and in ceremony
Are innocence and beauty born?
Ceremony's a name for the rich born
And custom for the spreading laurel tree.[56]

The sounds of the linnet are valuable for themselves, for the patterns in which they recur, rather than for their intellectual content. Hence the denunciation of "opinions" and of "an intellectual hatred." The alternative to this—Maude Gonne seen as an old bellows—exemplifies the opposite principle, the principle of party spirit that Pater denounces in "Two Early French Stories."[57] Custom, ceremony, and the linnet's song combine in a great chain of transmission; Yeats would have his daughter be one of the transmitters of the intricacies of her culture, without being committed to any cause or position.[58] Her spirit comes as "a prophecy of repose and simplicity." Like Marius, Florian Deleal, and the protagonists of *Imaginary Portraits*, "this character is a subtle blending and interpenetration of intellectual, moral, and spiritual elements"—in other words, the complex modern.[59]

Just as the Renaissance represents for Pater the

historical period of relativistic synthesis, so the Crystal Man represents the humanist apprehender. The individual apprehends and recreates or transmits the impressions he receives from outside himself. So Pater does in *The Renaissance,* and so does the *Mona Lisa,* the created epitome of the Renaissance. Pater is a subtle and complex enough esthetician to understand that the author, the created character, and the described work are but different manifestations of his Crystal Man, who, as spirit, may be (as in Yeats's "Byzantium")

> image, man or shade,
> Shade more than man, more image than a shade;

or

> Miracle, bird or golden handiwork,
> More miracle than bird or handiwork.[60]

And this Crystal Man is the apprehender that the "Conclusion" describes.

At the end of his essay on Michelangelo's poetry Pater states that one of the chief reasons for studying old masters is that old masters interpret and justify each other.[61] Victor Hugo and Blake, "though not of his school, and [significantly] unaware," interpret their predecessor Michelangelo, who in turn interprets them.[62] For Pater the whole body of created things exists, like music, as a continuing formal and non-metaphysical commentary on itself. Just as music—in its repetition of themes and its repeated variation of motifs that have been heard before—comments on its own content, so art—with its use of modern works as formal commentaries on older works and vice versa—comments on itself. The emphasis in Pater falls on form rather than on content; hence the comparison with music, which has no 'content' in the usual sense. It is for this reason that, as Pater asserts in "The School of Giorgione," all art aspires to the condition of music. The apprehension of the aspiration leads to his "Conclusion." That is, the apprehender (or Crystal Man) must, ideally, perceive the formal and nonmetaphysical nature of art. The apprehender works towards a perfection of apprehension in which he himself, like Yeats's narrator who goes to Byzantium, is transformed and becomes momentarily a part of the work of art he beholds. He perceives the formal movement of art and makes himself a part of it by the intensity of his perception.

Pater bases his contention that "all art constantly aspires towards the condition of music" on the perfect interpenetration of form and matter in music.[63] The degree to which the work of art attains the perfect interpenetration of form and matter within the limitations of its medium is the degree of its success: "this is what all art constantly strives after, and achieves in different degrees."[64] Pater acknowledges the different modes in which art attains its end:

> Each art, therefore, having its own peculiar and untranslatable sensuous charm, has its own special mode of reaching the imagination, its own special responsibilities to its material.[65]

He qualifies his acknowledgment of the distinctions, however, by noting the frequency with which the various forms of art work towards breaking through their individual limitations:

> Although each art has thus its own specific order of impressions, and an untranslatable charm, while

a just apprehension of the ultimate differences of
the arts is the beginning of aesthetic criticism; yet
it is noticeable that, in its special mode of handling
its given material, each art may be observed to
pass into the condition of some other art, by what
German critics term an *Anders-streben*—a partial
alienation from its own limitations, through which
the arts are able, not indeed to supply the place
of each other, but reciprocally to lend each other
new forces.[66]

The progression to the musical analogy becomes from
this point easy, and the extension of the argument to
the conditions of life itself follows. The interpenetration of form and matter makes art "independent of the
mere intelligence, to become a matter of pure perception."[67] So the ideal world of created and creating
things becomes like music.

Giorgione paints the men who listen—the ideal apprehenders. As a kind of Venetian examplar, Giorgione
is one of Pater's "unworldly" types. Venice remains
linked to its Byzantine beginnings, thus exemplifying
Pater's favorite culture, one in which each contemporary
expression of the spirit derives from or relates directly
to an earlier.[68] Giorgione had seemed to lose his historical identity because of the researches of Crowe and
Cavalcaselle.[69] Many of his paintings were assigned to
other artists, and the very existence of Giorgione as a
painter was challenged. Although Pater objected to
the destruction of the canon of Giorgione's work, he
found some satisfaction in the meager biographical details available about the painter.[70] Giorgione, even in
his lack of individuality, exists as an idea, a receptacle
of the spirit of Venice, "all that was intense or desirable
in it crystalising about the memory of this wonderful
young man."[71]

The crystalline Giorgione—image, man, or shade—shows us the great transmission of the pure perception that art strives to become:

> In these then, the favourite incidents of Giorgione's school, music or the musical intervals in our existence, life itself is conceived as a sort of listening—listening to music, to the reading of Bandello's novels, to the sound of water, to time as it flies.[72]

We may take the music to which Giorgione's painted folk listen to be the ideal complexity of perception, the synthesis of created things and natural beauty. Bandello's novels and the sound of water assume equal significance and blend into an affirmatively simple sound. Unity and simplicity would be the perceived ideal, expressed through the analogy of music. The lyres and lutes which La Gioconda hears, the sound of time as it flies, and Yeats's dance all become one to the ideal apprehender.

This ideal listener perceives his life as "a perpetual motion" of elemental forces.[73] He is the man spoken of and spoken to in the "Conclusion." The philosophy of the "Conclusion," far from being a *carpe diem* manifesto or a sermon of esthetic preciosity, simply directs the reader to seek ideal apprehension of the work of art and of the movement of life itself, to listen, to be aware of the "perpetual motion." Given Pater's description of the world as a place of subtly interpenetrating ideas, spirits, created and creating things, one can hardly censure his advice to attend to the music. Pater does not distinguish sharply between life and art. The interpenetration of the two manifests itself in Pater's followers Wilde and Yeats. The apprehender conceives of life as a kind of formal movement, like art, and the transforming apprehension makes any distinction of little value. Perhaps one reason for Pater's fondness for the liturgy is that in it the distinction between life and art becomes blurred and indeed disappears. Ideally we perceive "a magic web woven through and through us."[74] The complexity of this "magic web" reminds us of the Crystal Man, whose sensibilities are sharpened to such a point that he can apprehend complexity more completely than can the man of less acute sensibilities. The Crystal Man himself knows well how to "burn with a hard, gemlike flame."

"To burn always with this hard, gemlike flame, to maintain this ecstasy, is success in life."[75] The ecstasy derives from the act of perception. In the act of perception the Crystal Man, the ideal apprehender of the "Conclusion," is supreme. He sees "the external circumstances as they are"; thus art is for him like the art of the "Conclusion": it exists "for its own sake." And the image of crystal which Pater uses in "Diaphaneitè" fits nicely into the argument of the "Conclusion," published first as part of a review article on William Morris's poetry in the *Westminster Review* in October 1868, and in *The Renaissance* in 1873. The image of crystal, much resembling that of the gemlike flame, comprehends in itself both sound and light. The crystal responds to the motions of the air around it or to touch with sound, and it responds to light with reflected and enhanced light. And an inner light, perhaps the image of the listener's contribution to the music or of the flame's color adding to the light, leaps out to join the light without. For this gemlike flame and the Crystal Man are, as Pater says in "Diaphaneitè," "lighted up by some spiritual ray within."[76] The theme and the imagery run through Pater's work. The effect often is one of synesthesia, since Pater uses the flame and musical imagery almost interchangeably at times. Pico, the ideal humanist, exists as Crystal Man through the "glow and vehemence in his words which remind one of the manner in which his own brief existence flamed itself away."[77] And Yeats's voyager to Byzantium becomes part of the golden mosaic he perceives by the disinterested intensity of his apprehension of it. The crystalline light of pure, disinterested perception ultimately draws the perceiver, like Pico and Yeats's voyager, into the artifice of eternity.

Yeats may or may not have thought of Pater and his "Conclusion" when he wrote "Byzantium." But Pater's intellectual disciple does translate his mentor's dicta into artistic terms. The completeness of the apprehender's union with the work of art finds expression through the image of the flame:

> At midnight on the Emperor's pavement flit
> Flames that no faggot feeds, nor steel has lit,
> Nor storm disturbs, flames begotten of flame,
> Where blood-begotten spirits come
> And all complexities of fury leave,
> Dying into a dance,
> An agony of trance,
> An agony of flame that cannot singe a sleeve.

The Critic of Form

To discriminate schools, or art, of literature, is, of course, part of the obvious
business of literary criticism: but, in the
work of literary production, it is easy to
be overmuch occupied concerning them.
For, in truth, the legitimate contention is,
not of one age or school of literary art
against another, but of all successive
schools alike, against the stupidity which
is dead to the substance, and the vulgarity
which is dead to the form.

Pater, *Appreciations*

Pater's claim to a place among the greatest of modern lies in his particular understanding of form. It is hard to think of Pater as a formal critic—we are too beset by the genial essayist of many a country bibliophile's devotion, by the dreamy evocateur of literary anthologies, or by the deviant and unproductive recluse of efficient histories of criticism. But for the twentieth century, Pater may well be the most relevant of the Victorian critics. We can understand him. His concerns are our concerns. His approach to art is very much our approach and is applicable to art forms (cinema, for example) that did not exist in Pater's own time.

It takes no great analytic ability to see Pater as a synthesist, his predominant role as a historian of culture. Yet the synthesizing which Pater does goes repeatedly unnoticed, ignored in weary discussion about prose cadences. (Not that Pater's prose lacks cadence. Cadence abounds. But, from Saintsbury to the present, cadence has been the stopping point.) Even in his most comprehensive attempts to bring before his reader's mental eye the complexities of a period—*The Renaissance, Marius the Epicurean, Gaston de Latour*—Pater directs our attention beyond the particulars of the cultural synthesis and to their realization in the individual man, in the image of the human form.

In "Aesthetic Poetry," the other part of the essay from which the "Conclusion" to *The Renaissance* is taken and one of his most explicit statements of esthetic principles, Pater describes the medieval religious passion:

> In the *château,* the reign of reverie set in. The devotion of the cloister knew that mood thor-

35

oughly, and had sounded all its stops. For the object of this devotion was absent or veiled, not limited to one supreme plastic form like Zeus at Olympia or Athena in the Acropolis, but distracted, as in a fever dream, into a thousand symbols and reflections. But then, the Church, that new Sibyl, had a thousand secrets to make the absent near. Into this kingdom of reverie, and with it into a paradise of ambitious refinements, the earthly love enters, and becomes a prolonged somnambulism. Of religion it learns the art of directing towards an unseen object sentiments whose natural direction is towards objects of sense. Hence a love defined by the absence of the beloved, choosing to be without hope, protesting against all lower uses of love, barren, extravagant, antinomian. It is the love which is incompatible with marriage, for the chevalier who never comes, of the serf for the châtelaine, of the rose for the nightingale, of Rudel for the Lady of Tripoli. Another element of extravagance came in with the feudal spirit: Provençal love is full of the very forms of vassalage. To be the servant of love, to have offended, to taste the subtle luxury of chastisement, of reconciliation—the religious spirit, too, knows that, and meets just there, as in Rousseau, the delicacies of the earthly love. Here, under this strange complex of conditions, as in some medicated air, exotic flowers of sentiment expand, among people of a remote and unaccustomed beauty, somnambulistic, frail, androgynous, the light almost shining through them. Surely, such loves were too fragile and adventurous to last more than a moment.[1]

• Like much of Pater, the passage is best known for the wrong reasons—the familiar part is the reference to "frail, androgynous" people, usually taken, probably rightly, as an indication of Pater's own sexual preference. The paragraph that follows, however, tends to undercut what has gone before:

> That monastic religion of the Middle Age was, in fact, in many of its bearings, like a beautiful disease or disorder of the sense: and a religion which is a disorder of the senses must always be subject to illusions. Reverie, illusion, delirium: they are the three stages of a fatal descent both in the religion and the loves of the Middle Age.[2]

Although Pater acknowledges three stages of "a fatal descent," we have one of the common instances of his evading the obvious. The process of the fatal descent clearly fascinated him and he uses it as an analogy for the desirable response in his own time to works of art. The historical distance, the seemingly pejorative language, and the escape (after the sentence ending "the loves of the Middle Age") into a discussion of Victor Hugo serve the public purpose of obfuscation, while the private purpose of being consistent with his stated esthetic principles remains perfectly clear to those who read closely enough and with a suspension of their own presuppositions about his intent.

In his best apologetic manner, Pater manages to turn a discussion of religion into a discussion of unconsummated physical love, and the ease with which his analysis can be applied to art justifies Eliot's strictures about art replacing religion in Pater. But Eliot does not face completely the implications of Pater's criticism, probably because Eliot concerns himself particularly with *Marius* and does not consider relevant parts of "Aesthetic Poetry" and the "Postscript" to *Apprecia-*

tions. In "Aesthetic Poetry," Pater does give us a religious ecstasy that is essentially "aesthetic," a response to the human image in art. But the ecstasy always comes from a joining of the religious sensation with the physical sensation, resulting in an estheticism made up of one part religious fervor and one part erotic impulse. If, for the Middle Ages, religion "learns the art of directing towards an unseen object sentiments whose natural direction is towards objects of sense," then Pater carries the process a step further for his own time: he redirects towards images of art those sentiments that religion had once won for itself. Thus we see Pater as the critic playing priest, his religion being an art catholic, an art that embraces many modes but demands a response at once sensuous and contemplative.

Interestingly enough, Pater works towards establishing a distinction between the Greek worship of a physical image (Zeus of Olympia, for example) and the medieval worship of an unseen diety, manifested almost fantastically in a profusion of light and symbol. ("Aesthetic Poetry" goes far to explain Pater's fondness for liturgy—the manifestation of the object of worship in ceremony and in suggestive image is surely implied.) For a resolution of the two conflicting modes of worship, Pater falls back on his image of the Crystal Man. The Zeus of Olympia and the "thousand symbols and reflections" come together in the "people of a remote and unaccustomed beauty, somnambulistic, frail, androgynous, the light almost shining through them." The object of the votary's worship is both human image and shimmering reflection, a complex of symbols and light penetrating and indistinct from the human form they inhabit. By ending his description with the comment that such worship could last only for a moment, Pater is not so much constructing a literary tradition as indicating that the esthetic application of his analysis can only be a fleeting thing. The "moments" of the "Conclusion" are, for the converted, exceptionally precious. Making them last or recreating them or accumulating as many as possible lies beyond the competence of the individual and is the work of the body of artists and critics who create, recreate, and transmit the images that others worship. As the priest who directs the votary towards his object of worship, the critic seeks to identify new images to fill the moments of his initiates. Such was Pater's task.

As the guide to the would-be esthetic votary, Pater acts as a synthesist whose usual vehicle is the human image. Pater offers the most sustained example of his criticism in *The Renaissance,* where the focus is repeatedly on various historical personages or on the human image as it comes to us in the art of the period. Pater's synthesis excludes only by omission, intentional and accidental, and its comprehensiveness argues for the validity of the critic's relativistic viewpoint. Pater treats his ideal critic—and votary—Winckelmann as a connecting point between critical theory and appreciation, as well as between the Renaissance and the nineteenth century. For Pater, Winckelmann exemplifies the modern humanist, the heir of Pico, who can respond sensuously to a work of art.

Pater's criticism repeatedly emphasizes variety and contradiction in art, largely because the critic's aim is to inculcate catholicity of taste, even when, as in the "Preface" to *The Renaissance,* he speaks of discrimination. In fact, Pater seeks more to define how we should respond to works of art than to give detailed analyses. He wants those who follow his dicta to expand their sympathies, to become relativists, to be able to achieve some degree of religious and sensuous delight from works of art that come from cultures different from their own.

One of the aims of Pater's catholicity of taste is to interest his reader: the variety serves as an inducement to accept the whole. Thus to lead his reader to an impassioned appreciation of the work of art, Pater strives to give the work as broad an appeal as possible. This leads him to deemphasize the traditional sets of opposites upon which most critics depend. When Pater discusses seemingly opposing ideological or critical positions, it is only to demonstrate how they are really the same thing. This aspect of his critical theory finds typical expression in the "Postscript" to *Appreciations.*[3] Like the "Preface" and "Conclusion" to *The Renaissance,* the "Postscript"—with the later-dropped "Aesthetic Poetry"—provides a framework for the accompanying essays and offers a more explicit introduction to Pater's theory than any of the individual selections, including the essay "Style."

The "Postscript" deals with the distinctions between classic and romantic. Pater defines the terms with little specific reference to history, although he does generally associate classicism with the ancient world and romanticism with the modern.

> The "classic" comes to us out of the cool and quiet of other times, as the measure of what a long experience has shown will at least never displease us. And in the classical literature of Greece and Rome, as in the classics of the last century, the essentially classical element is that quality of order in beauty, which they possess, indeed, in a preeminent degree, and which impresses some minds to the exclusion of everything else in them.[4]

The definition of romantic is completely nonhistorical and Pater expands the definition of classic to include the romantic temper.

> It is the addition of strangeness to beauty, that constitutes the romantic character in art; and the desire of beauty being a fixed element in every artistic organisation, it is the addition of curiosity to this desire of beauty, that constitutes the romantic temper.[5]

Pater comes perilously close to suggesting that strangeness is nothing less than novelty. But a more sympathetic reading reveals that strangeness is more the element of striking departure from the norm of art as it is known in any one period. Thus Beethoven's later symphonies are romantic in their departure from familiar eighteenth-century norms of symphonic construction. And Sheridan's comedies would be classic in their close adherence to the eighteenth-century English dramatic mode, although it might be argued that the latter example applies only in retrospect. Where the norms are not strict, then all art may be romantic—as, for Pater, most "modern" art is.

Pater's definitions, for all their derivation from French contemporaries, from Goethe, and from eighteenth- and early nineteenth-century English theory, had their impact largely because they employ Pater's best assertive and suggestive style. As with Pater's other writings, however, the distinctions between romantic and classical are far less important for the theory and practice of his criticism than the similarities. For the synthesizing relativist, the common bases of any two ideas are more important than the distinctions; at least for Pater, the emphasis is on compatibility, not contrariety.

In defining the terms, Pater establishes the common

foundation upon which they rest. Since the classic represents "order in beauty" and the romantic represents
"the addition of strangeness to beauty," the "fixed
element in every artistic organisation" is "the desire of
beauty." Pater does not clarify what he means by "the
desire of beauty." Probably, however, he means that
the object satisfies the beholder's craving for perfect
form, however, momentarily. The desire of beauty may
well be the power to arouse the combination of religious
and sensuous fervor of which Pater speaks in "Aesthetic Poetry." The romantic addition would then be
the expanding body of subject matter and the varying
ways of depicting it available to the artist in an increasingly relativistic modern age. John Bayley defines
Pater's aim well:

> The Paterian solution [to the Romantic predica-
> ment] is neither a retreat into the mind nor an
> attempt to enter the phenomena of the external
> world, but a frank assertion that the mind's suc-
> cessive *aperçus,* its privileged moments when it is
> in harmony with what it perceives, and burns (in
> the notorious phrase) with a hard gem-like flame—
> these are what is worth having, and when they
> occur in the artist's experience they can be trans-
> mitted to, or rather picked up by, his audience. . . .
> The poet is not "a man speaking to men," but a
> man whose consciousness is open to the public if
> they are interested.[6]

The beholder's "privileged moments," then, are the
moments when he exists in harmony with what he
beholds. Like the Crystal Man, the beholder—the votary
—reflects and perhaps even becomes momentarily part
of the image he beholds. Since, for Pater's purposes,
the materials to which the beholder responds are varied,

his response leads to a complexity of character like that defined in the "Conclusion" to *The Renaissance.*

A possible oneness of the apprehender and the work of art apprehended appeals to Pater's synthesizing mind because of its implications about the act of perception. Just as the work of art perceived brings to the apprehender the full train of associations which it has acquired by historical accident or by internal balance (insofar as these can be apprehended by the individual), so the apprehender brings to the work of art his own particular sensibility with its conditioned responses. The element each individual work of art presumably has in common with other works of art, is that is satisfies "the desire of beauty"; it aids the perceiver's movement towards perfect form, towards oneness with the perceived. (The added "strangeness" of the romantic work of art does not, of course, interfere with the movement towards oneness.) The resultant vision partakes of two trains of association coming together and reinforcing each other.

So for Pater both classic and romantic art endeavor to give the beholder a desire to attain oneness with the work. This mutually-held characteristic makes the distinction between classic and romantic less significant. The argument of the "Postscript" works to temper rather than to emphasize the difference. Pater opens the "Postscript" with a criticism of the overly strict exclusiveness of strongly-held romantic and classic opinions:

> Used in an exaggerated sense, to express a greater opposition between these tendencies than really exists, they have at times tended to divide people of taste into opposite camps. But in that *House Beautiful,* which the creative minds of all generations—the artists and those who have treated life

> in the spirit of art—are always building together, for the refreshment of the human spirit, these oppositions cease; and the *Interpreter* of the *House Beautiful,* the true aesthetic critic, uses these divisions, only so far as they enable him to enter into the peculiarities of the objects with which he has to do.[7]

As in "The School of Giorgione," he does not attack historical or generic criticism, but he does emphasize the synthetic nature of his own effort. In "The School of Giorgione" Pater argues for the aspiration of all the arts to the formal condition of music, that is, for the breaking-down of distinctions between the various artistic modes, an effect which Pater himself seems to achieve in his essentially pictorial prose. Similarly, and on a narrower level, he argues in "Style" for less strict distinctions between romanticism and classicism. And in "Dante Gabriel Rossetti," he writes of another merging of concepts we have traditionally thought of as separate: "Spirit and matter, indeed, have been for the most part opposed, with a false contrast or antagonism by schoolmen, whose artificial creation those abstractions really are. In our actual concrete experience, the two trains of phenomena which the words *matter* and *spirit* do but roughly distinguish, play inextricably into each other."[8]

In "Two Early French Stories" Pater asserts, as already noted, that both the Renaissance men, such as Abelard, and the saints have a place in the House Beautiful. He implies that beauty derives in part from the inclusiveness. Pater's House Beautiful is complex, relativistic—an extension to include the pagan of the "palace called Beautiful" in *Pilgrim's*

Progress. In his essay on Wordsworth, Pater notes that St. Catherine of Siena

> has won for herself an undying place in the *House Beautiful,* not by her rectitude of soul only, but by its "fairness"—by those quite different qualities which commend themselves to the poet and the artist.[9]

The House Beautiful has both order in beauty and added strangeness; it includes all that can be perceived.

The "Postscript" gives a more comprehensive series of examples in support of its argument than is usual for Pater. Blake, for instance, becomes for Pater the "born romantic" in a classical period. But the synthesizing spirit goes beyond the insertion of romantics in classical slots. In fact, Pater effectively denies the intrinsic classicism of any work:

> All critical terms are relative; and there is at least a valuable suggestion in that theory of Stendhal's, that all good art was romantic in its day. In the beauties of Homer and Pheidias, quiet as they now seem, there must have been, for those who confronted them for the first time, excitement and surprise, the sudden, unforeseen satisfaction of the desire of beauty. Yet the *Odyssey,* with its marvelous adventure, is more romantic than the *Iliad,* which nevertheless contains, among many other romantic episodes, that of the immortal horses of Achilles, who weep at the death of Patroclus. Aeschylus is more romantic than Sophocles, whose *Philoctetes,* were it written now, might figure, for the strangeness of its execution, as typically romantic; while, of Euripides, it may be said, that his method in writing his plays is to sacrifice

45

readily almost everything else, so that he may attain the fulness of a single romantic effect. These two tendencies, indeed, might be applied as a measure or standard through Greek and Roman art and poetry, with very illuminating results; and for an analyst of the romantic principle in art, no exercise would be more profitable, than to walk through the collection of classical antiquities at the Louvre, or the British Museum, or to examine some representative collection of Greek coins, and note how the element of curiosity, of the love of strangeness, insinuates itself into classical design, and record the effects of the romantic spirit there, the traces of struggle of the grotesque even, though overbalanced here by sweetness; as in the sculpture of Chartres and Rheims, the real sweetness of mind in the sculptor is often overbalanced by the grotesque, by the rudeness of strength.[10]

Pater argues, almost paradoxically, his contention that classic and romantic elements coexist in great art—that all masterworks have both, even if the predominance of one or the other seems more evident because of the historical moment at which the work is being analyzed.

The passage exhibits Pater's synthesizing skill. Seemingly intractable material fits nicely into the argument. He acknowledges that classicism is a term which may signify antiquity more than any other distinctive quality. The unstated argument might assume that the familiarity of the work of art—gained as the work becomes known to new generations as an artifact—leads to an appreciation of its "order in beauty" and makes its "strangeness" seem less strange. Pater might be said to believe that any age which views ideas relativistically is an age of romanticism, a modern age; yet as the products of the age gain years and reputation, they no longer seem strange but become classic. *Philoctetes,* for example, seems ordered and classical merely because of its familiarity. Admittedly, Pater does try to make all classical art romantic. The critical intent, however, is to unite what is divided, and Pater as a romantic critic assessing classical materials makes them fit his own evaluative criteria. Pater notes that for Stendhal, "all good art is romantic."[11] And the distinction which Stendhal makes between the romantic and a narrow and pedantic classicism pervades Pater's essay in a modified form. Pater insists that the possibility of a warm and sensuous response to a work of art should never be avoided:

> [*Classical*] has often been used in a hard, and merely scholastic sense, by the praisers of what is old and accustomed, at the expense of what is new, by critics who would never have discovered for themselves the charm of any work, whether new or old, who value what is old, in art or literature, for its accessories, and chiefly for the conventional authority that has gathered about it—people who would never really have been made glad by any Venus fresh risen from the sea, and who praise the Venus of old Greece and Rome, only because they fancy her grown now into something staid and tame.[12]

The effort to synthesize, however, serves no ideology of esthetics. It serves, rather, the very practical purpose of making classicism more attractive by citing its romantic components. For the late-nineteenth-century public, romanticism induced a readier response than classicism—even if the response might be a negative one. In any case, a belief in the response a romantic work

47

could induce is one of Pater's critical assumptions, however much his own reputation suffered because of his particular vein of romanticism. As in other instances, Pater fights the same battle as Arnold, in this case on behalf of classicism. But whereas Arnold's weapon is his restrained and studied praise of classic art, Pater's is his redefinition of it in *Appreciations* and his sensuous response to the classic in *Plato and Platonism* and *Greek Studies.*

Pater's method of making art seem attractive to a contemporary audience follows from his method of interpreting specific works. The associativeness of Pater's prose allows the reader to bring a fuller response to the work of art than would have been possible without it. To achieve a critical mode in which the reader's full associative powers will be brought to bear upon his response to the work, Pater uses a widely suggestive critical vocabulary. The implications of the criticism go far beyond any strict group of terms. Pater manages to give the terms he uses a definition in context which, if not especially limited, does serve his purposes as synthetic critic.

The suggestive critical vocabulary manifests itself throughout the Pater canon. Witness a central passage on Botticelli:

> He is before all things a poetical painter, blending the charm of story and sentiment, the medium of the art of poetry, with the charm of line and colour, the medium of abstract painting. So he becomes the illustrator of Dante.[13]

Interestingly enough, the assertion that Botticelli is a "poetical painter"—by which Pater means a narrative painter and therefore a painter of men—fastens itself upon the mind and becomes the focal point of Pater's analysis. And a continuing investigation of the passage shows some very specific points of reference in the Botticelli style to support the assertion and indeed to define the term "poetical painter."

> Botticelli's illustrations are crowded with incident, blending, with a naïve carelessness of pictorial propriety, three phases of the same scene into one plate. . . . in the scene of those who "go down quick into hell," there is an inventive force about the fire taking hold on the upturned soles of the feet, which proves that the design is no mere translation of Dante's words, but a true painter's vision; . . . [in] the scene of the Centaurs . . . Botticelli has gone off with delight on the thought of the Centaurs themselves, bright, small creatures of the woodland, with arch baby faces and mignon forms, drawing tiny bows.[14]

The impact of the detailed analysis can hardly be denied, for the support that Pater gives to his initial assertion that Botticelli's work is "poetical" lends precision to a seemingly vague terminology. Pater makes an interesting connection between narrative style and the linear quality of some Florentine art (as noted before Pater by Wölfflin and others) which indicates both a high degree of critical acumen and a hard core of skillfully disguised common sense. An initially vague assertion gains precision through specific illustration, and yet the effect of suggestive terminology remains powerful.

Pater arrives at his definition of Botticelli's *via media* from the initial demonstration of his qualities as narrative painter. The resulting argument follows this general course: 1) Botticelli employs a narrative and linear style in his illustrations of Dante[15]; 2) but Botticelli is not a "mere naturalist" in an age of naturalists; 3) Botticelli lets his "interest" work upon the narrative of Dante (with its "insoluble element of prose"); 4) Botticelli draws an appreciative representation of those wistful "exiles" whom Dante scorns "as unworthy alike of heaven and hell"; 5) the "middle world" which Botticelli accepts and Dante seems to reject is to some extent for Pater the most attractive part of the humanist's approach to experience, the morality of it being "all sympathy." Botticelli's virtue is his delineation of "men and women, in their mixed and uncertain condition." Pater's evocation of Botticelli's *via media* stands as perhaps the most influential part of his art criticism, save for the passage describing the *Mona Lisa*.[16] The evocation derives from a close description of Botticelli's work; the associative mode of reasoning should not disguise the soundness of Pater's analysis, particularly since only through the associative mode can Pater attain the complexity he desires.

The famous passage from the essay on Leonardo which discusses the *Mona Lisa* stands apart, both as the most distinctive example of Pater's associative method and as the *bête noire* of later critics, the purple passage in which Pater's imagination supposedly allows itself to wander far from its subject into the recesses of his own mind.[17] The focus remains on the human image, the critical approach is synthetic, and the argument is associative.

> The presence that rose thus so strangely beside the waters, is expressive of what in the ways of a thousand years men had come to desire. Hers is the head upon which all "the ends of the world are

come," and the eyelids are a little weary. It is a beauty wrought out from within upon the flesh, the deposit, little cell by cell, of strange thoughts and fantastic reveries and exquisite passions. Set it for a moment beside one of those white Greek goddesses or beautiful women of antiquity, and how would they be troubled by this beauty, into which the soul with all its maladies has passed! All the thoughts and experience of the world have etched and moulded there, in that which they have of power to refine and make expressive the outward form, the animalism of Greece, the lust of Rome, the mysticism of the middle age with its spiritual ambition and imaginative loves, the return of the Pagan world, the sins of the Borgias. She is older than the rocks among which she sits; like the vampire, she has been dead many times, and learned the secrets of the grave; and has been a diver in deep seas, and keeps their fallen day about her; and trafficked for strange webs with Eastern merchants, and, as Leda, was the mother of Helen of Troy, and, as Saint Anne, the mother of Mary; and all this has been to her but as the sound of lyres and flutes, and lives only in the delicacy with which it has moulded the changing lineaments, and tinged the eyelids and the hands. The fancy of a perpetual life, sweeping together ten thousand experiences, is an old one; and modern philosophy has conceived the idea of humanity as wrought upon by, and summing up in itself, all modes of thought and life. Certainly Lady Lisa might stand as the embodiment of the old fancy, the symbol of the modern idea.[18]

The uniqueness of the passage as criticism lies in its power to awaken the memory, to sharpen the sensibility, to evoke the qualities of the *Mona Lisa* by a complex

Walter Pater

group of associations that are usually valid from the art-historical point of view. For Pater the *Mona Lisa* comprehends in herself the complex and varied intellectual forces at work in the Renaissance. The sources of her face lie in both the Virgins of the High Gothic churches and the Venuses of the Hellenic age. As Saint Anne she is Gothic Virgin and as Leda she is Hellenic sculpture. She exists as both simultaneously and alternatively so that she has been Saint Anne without being Leda and Leda without being Saint Anne; yet for the modern, who must perceive, in his post-Renaissance position, the full complexity of the world she inhabits, she is both. The analogy to music suggests the unchanging nature of the work in its essential being: the varying associations brought to bear upon the *Mona Lisa* by its apprehenders affect the artifact itself not at all. The "sound of lyres" represents the cultural stream that Pater defines for us in the passage.

One has only to inspect some of Leonardo's drawings and the painting to understand how much the *Mona Lisa* is both Saint Anne and Leda. Pater's essay indicates that he had seen enough of the paintings of the school of Leonardo to recognize in the *Mona Lisa* the motifs with which the artist worked. The complex experience Leonardo brought to the painting finds summation in Pater. Of the passage Sir Kenneth Clark writes: "The English critic, above all, is embarrassed by Pater's immortal passage ringing in his ears, and reminding him that anything he may write will be poor and shallow by comparison."[19] In Pater's description of the *Mona Lisa,* apprehender and work of art meet and attain oneness—a oneness which is preserved in Pater's prose. If we cannot see the features right, it is not because our eyes have been misdirected.

The Critic of Form

Pater's associative method has a specific technical source. In this passage he uses words and phrases having general connotations, such as "spiritual ambition and imaginative loves" and "a diver in deep seas," and he uses allusions having a veiled quality about them—"the animalism of Greece, the lust of Rome, . . . the return of the Pagan world, the sins of the Borgias." Pater's choice of words does smack of cheap historical novels, but behind the cheapness lies the motive of interesting the viewer in the work of art. The historical novel is self-sufficient; Pater's essay recreates visual image. And Pater's more bizarre associations do represent the element of strangeness added to beauty as he perceives it.

But another element in Pater's prose goes far towards making the reader feel that a faint memory of something known before has been aroused. That element is a modulated repetition. Pater repeats, with very slight changes, certain words and phrases: sweetness, comely, *ex forti dulcedo,* languor. After working through several of the essays in *The Renaissance* or *Appreciations,* the reader begins to sense an almost liturgical repetition of certain elements in the prose with only the slightest modification. One notes the modulation of phrase and idea, each faintly evocative of another because of an understated repetition.

Pater's repetition is a carefully controlled device. We have to read only a little Pater to become familiar with Leda and Helen, with *ex forti dulcedo,* with the "intimate impress of indwelling souls," with pure form, and with the flame. In the use of slightly reworded ideas and in the repetition of words and allusions, Pater conveys a total impression, just as music does in the repetition of slightly varied themes. The unity of *The Renaissance,* for example, bears analogy to the unity of some great works of music: both depend on repetition that varies the theme slightly each time it is repeated. (The same might be said of *Greek Studies* and *Plato and Platonism. Appreciations* has less coherence of purpose and repetition does not serve so clearly to unify the volume.) Furthermore, themes are repeated in different contexts, and thereby connect different bodies of intellectual material by applying the same mode of expression to each. Witness Pater's use of what we may call the "moment of vision" motif as he applies it to a sudden intellectual illumination, whether in responsee to a work of art or in response to life:

> In these then, the favourite incidents of Giorgione's school, music or the musical interval in our existence, life is conceived as a sort of listening. . . . Often such moments are our moments of play, and we are surprised at the unexpected blessedness of what may seem our least important part of time.[20]

> A sudden light transfigures some trivial thing, a weathervane, a windmill, a winnowing fan, the dust in the barn door. A moment—and the thing has vanished, because it was pure effect; but it leaves a relish behind it, a longing that the accident may happen again.[21]

> And if we continue to dwell in thought on this world, not of objects in the solidity with which language invests them, but of impressions, unstable, flickering, inconsistent, which burn and are extinguished with our consciousness of them, it contracts still further.[22]

The repetition of theme consists in these passages of a repeated use of particular words, such as "moment"

The Critic of Form

(the small fragment which when compounded forms experience), and of particular images, such as that of light; it also consists in applying what, for want of a better critical term, one may call a motif. This "moment of vision" motif imposes itself first on the subject matter of a work of art; second, on an experience caused by the natural action of light; and finally, on the whole range of sensually apprehended experience. Repetition of word, image, allusion, and motif constitutes a repetition of theme, and this repetition of theme gives *The Renaissance* part of its unity. The evocative element in Pater's prose asserts itself as a unifying force that gives stylistic coherence to *The Renaissance*. At the same time it gives the reader a sense of dimly remembered experience that Pater wants so much to convey. At some point the reader begins to think that Pater's motif is a part of the reader's own experience—that he, the reader, has experience what he has, in fact, only read in Pater.

For Pater, the critic's part in building the House Beautiful or in leading converts to it involves extending the range of associations which the beholder brings to the work of art. Thus the cabalistic associations of the *Mona Lisa*. The extended range of associations serves to increase the relevance of the work of art to the beholder, to make the oneness for which the beholder should strive easier to attain. The "genius by accumulation" which Pater describes in "Raphael" may belong in some degree to the apprehender as well as to the creator. Accumulation makes oneness easier.[23]

"To turn always with that ever-changing spirit, yet to retain the flavour of what was admirably done in past generations . . . is the problem of true romantic-

55

ism."[24] Pater's ideal apprehender and critic Winckelmann approaches this problem—perhaps even solves it.
(Winckelmann belongs in any discussion of romanticism, since the term "true romanticism" may be understood nonhistorically as Pater uses it in the "Postscript.")
Aware of his mortality and eager to unite himself with
the world of things-to-be-apprehended, Winckelmann
fits nicely into Pater's framework. He represents the
modern beset by spiritual emptiness who endeavors to
satisfy himself through the apprehension of art.

The modernity which Winckelmann represents is
the modernity central to Pater's description of the
Mona Lisa. Pater speaks of the effect that "this beauty
into which the soul with all its maladies had passed"
would have had upon the Greek goddesses, representa-
tives as they were of a unified civilization. What
Burckhardt had said of the Italian of the Renaissance—
that "he was the first-born among the sons of modern
Europe"[25]—finds an eloquent and probably independent
confirmation in Pater's passage on Leonardo's painting:
"Lady Lisa might stand as the embodiment of the old
fancy, the symbol of the modern idea." That is, in her
combination of Christian and pagan, the *Mona Lisa*,
like the Italian of the Renaissance in Burckhardt, is a
modern. Her consoling power is in her full apprehension of the stream of experience through which she
has passed.

This "modern idea," this "soul with all its maladies,"
resembles the quality of "sweetness" upon which Pater
frequently insists. The "modern idea" of which he
speaks may be defined as the awareness of the self as
a transient entity and the recognition of the flux that
is so much a quality of all life. It is the inwardness of
Christianity deprived of its supernatural supports.

Wordsworth had stated the problem best fifty years before Pater: because of the transiency of the self we "long for a repose that ever is the same." The malaise that besets the post-Christian man bothered the Greek little, at least for Pater's purposes as cultural historian. "Sweetness" is the apprehension in the work of art of the modern idea—the paradoxical arresting of the idea of the self as a transient entity. The necessary awareness of the transitory nature of the self lies at the very heart of Pater's argument in *The Renaissance*. Pater concerns himself with certain works of art that most show this awareness.

The most satisfactory statement of the awareness comes in the essay on Winckelmann:

> This pagan sentiment measures the sadness with which the human mind is filled, whenever its thoughts wander far from what is here, and now. It is beset by notions of irresistible natural powers, for the most part ranged against man, but the secret also of his fortune, making the earth golden and the grape fiery for him. He makes gods in his own image, gods smiling and flower-crowned, or bleeding by some sad fatality, to console him by their wounds, never closed from generation to generation. It is with a rush of home-sickness that the thought of death presents itself. He would remain at home for ever on the earth if he could.[26]

Pater clearly dissociates the "pagan sentiment" from any one religion (and "pagan sentiment" is not equivalent to "sweetness") but in the same passage defines it as the "broad foundation" for all religions, including Christianity. We are thrown back to the brooding Gioconda, and we become aware of her embodiment of the "pagan sentiment," itself "the soul with all its maladies." As the foundation for all religions, the "pagan sentiment" must be embodied in both Christianity and in the religion of the Greeks.

One of the principal problems in understanding *The Renaissance* and therefore Winckelmann lies in determining the relationship between "the old fancy" and "the modern idea." How does the Greek ideal link itself to the Christian ideal in the Renaissance to produce "the modern idea"? A solution along the following lines may be suggested: A pagan sentiment which embodies both the pleasure of life and the concern with death definies itself as the basis for both the Greek religion (or unity of culture) and the Christian religion. For the Greeks, the sentiment manifested itself as an apprehension of the present, of the daily quality of life, with little thought of the passage of time and of last things. In Christianity, the sentiment directs the thought of the living towards eschatology, placing little emphasis on the pleasures of life itself. In the Renaissance man, in Leonardo and his *Mona Lisa,* the pagan sentiment becomes again a unified thing; Christian man returns to Greek culture and from it derives a sense of the pleasures of man in his earthly state. The Renaissance Christian becomes, to use the term loosely, a humanist, and in doing so, he also becomes modern man—with a dichotomy of feeling, apprehending the importance of death all the more for having been given a sense of the pleasure of life. Hence Pater's statement that the "sweetness" in Renaissance art comes from the Christian world's apprehension of the classical world, for it is only the union with the classical world that makes "sweetness" possible.[27]

Sweetness, *intimité, ex forti dulcedo* most precisely define the modern idea because they suggest a combination of classical and Christian motifs. In learning to enjoy the pleasures of the present moment, the Renaissance artist was forced to look beyond his Christian heritage to an idealized time in which the soul lived in perfect harmony with the body and in which no spiritual world contended with the world of the flesh. Embodying modernity in an early form as it does, the Renaissance serves as the perfect vehicle for Pater's thought: Renaissance art combines sweetness and strength and defines the modern idea.

> And to the true admirers of Michelangelo this is the true type of the Michelangelesque—sweetness and strength, pleasure with surprise, an energy of conception which seems at every moment about to break through all the conditions of comely form, recovering, touch by touch, a loveliness found usually only in the simplest natural things—*ex forti dulcedo*.[28]

Pater finds an analogous quality in the poetry of the troubadours, in the verse of du Bellay, in the paintings of Leonardo. Yet he distinguishes between those works and works which lack sweetness—that is, Greek sculpture:

> Fair as the young men of the Elgin marbles, the Adam of the Sistine Chapel is unlike them in a total absence of that balance and completeness which express so well the sentiment of a self-contained, independent life.[29]

For Pater, and for the Renaissance as he interprets it to us, the world of Greece embodies the "completeness, centrality" which the intellect demands. This completeness may be defined as the absence of subjectivity and completeness of apprehension, the oneness of the ancient with the physical life on earth.

> The Greek mind had advanced to a particular stage of self-reflexion, but was careful not to pass beyond it. . . . just there Greek thought finds its happy limit; it has not yet become too inward; the mind has not yet learned to boast its independence of the flesh.[30]

The Renaissance employs an unstated but persuasive analogy between the awareness of the self as a transient entity, which is the modern condition, and the endeavor of the quattrocento Italians to regain the unified culture of Greece. Modern man has an awareness of his own transiency as part of his Christian inheritance, but he has been deprived of the consolation that Christianity was once able to offer. The Renaissance inclination towards the state of mind that produced the *Venus of Melos,* "in no sense a symbol, a suggestion, of anything beyond its own victorious fairness,"[31] found itself turned inward by the Christian inheritance which had intervened between the Renaissance man and the stoic ideal.

Pater's solution to the problem he poses (or rather identifies, for the problem is implicit in the modern condition as he defines it) derives from his definition of humanism. In *The Renaissance* and in "Raphael," fullness of apprehension is the humanist virtue. The humanist has the comprehensive sympathy which the early medieval Christian, the Reformation minister, or the ideologue of the French Revolution may lack. Humanism implies a historical catholicity that eschews the specific period and works towards synthesis.

Pater's definition of humanism, given in his essay on Pico in *The Renaissance,* is quite specific:

> He [Pico] is a true *humanist.* For the essence of humanism is that belief of which he seems never to have doubted, that nothing which has ever interested living men and women can wholly lose its vitality—no language they have spoken, nor oracle beside which they have hushed their voices, no dream which has once been entertained by actual human minds, nothing about which they have ever been passionate, or expended time and zeal.[32]

The humanism which Pater offers as a response to the relativistic condition of the modern world must be understood somewhat differently from the humanism of Matthew Arnold, for example. Arnold's humanism includes a principle of selectivity—Arnold seeks "the best" that has been thought in setting up an authoritative tradition. Humanism, as traditionally understood, and as understood by Arnold, affirms a single valid tradition, based on Hellenic and Judeo-Christian origins and comprehending the "best" part of Western thought. Pater's humanism takes as its duty the preservation of everything that has interested living men. It includes whatever has moved men—not only the best; the assertion of some set of explicit values is notably absent in Pater's definition. Inclusion, recovery, and reconciliation characterize Pater's humanism.

The essay on Winckelmann offers a humanist solution to the problem of transiency, the instance of a modern man who in a sense represents the end of the Renaissance because he achieves the Renaissance ideal of a recovery, insofar as a recovery is possible, of the Greek spirit, of cultural unity. The portrait of Winckelmann, ironically, shows us an ideal, the whole man, only to make clearer the fact that the modern condition may prevent a return to the Hellenic ideal. Winckelmann, a historical freak, stands at the end of the Renaissance precisely because beyond him recovery may be impossible; with Goethe, modernity reigns unchallenged, and modernity in Goethe has been somehow brought forth in Germany under the influence of an antiquarian with Hellenic tastes, just as it had been brought forth in Italy by a contact with the culture of Greece, with Greek statues and manuscripts. Modern man may not, however, be able to recapture as fully as Winckelmann the rich complexity of the flux about him. Modern man, like Coleridge, will not settle for cultural relativism and seeks the absolute. The epigraph to the essay on Winckelmann, with all its associations, drives home the point of the essay: *Et ego in Arcadia fui.* The tombstone inscription, bringing back the image of the dead shepherd in Poussin's painting, stands as a postscript to the life of Winckelmann, reminding modern man that if Winckelmann has been in Arcadia, then all the more reason that modern man cannot be.

Winckelmann becomes both the Renaissance man and the Attic hero, translated into modern terms:

> The element of affinity which he [Plato] presents to Winckelmann is that which is wholly Greek, and alien from the Christian world, represented by that group of brilliant youths in the Lysis, still uninfected by any spiritual sickness, finding the end of all endeavour in the aspects of the human form, the continual stir and motion of a comely human life.[33]

Pater's ideal of the modern Attic hero in Winckelmann is sound enough for the reader to understand that

Pater has few illusions about the culture of Greece being any less self-conscious than modern culture. It is not, for the Olympians do think beyond their own "victorious fairness":

> The placid minds even of Olympian Gods are troubled with thoughts of a limit of duration, of inevitable decay, of dispossession.[34]

The ideal of an Attic lack of self-consciousness is necessary, even as the ideal of Winckelmann is necessary; had the Greeks been very self-conscious, we should have had to deny it. The cultural unity of Greece may be compared to the house in which Florian Deleal passes his childhood or to the "White-nights" of Marius. Greece serves the function of mythical-historical Eden and Winckelmann's striving after the unity it seems to offer indicates that he has to some extent solved the problem of the flux. In his apprehension of the Renaissance synthesis, particularly of its Attic or edenic components, he attains the satisfaction which comforts Marius at his death. Winckelmann looms before us as the ideal votary; his example directs us to achieve as much vital consciousness of the flow of ideas about us as possible. The example of Winckelmann, indeed, provides for the modern the edenic time-before that makes the effort to apprehend seem less hopeless. And as in *Marius* and *Imaginary Portraits,* senuous and spiritual response to "the aspects of the human form" becomes the humanist solution to the problem of transiency.

In "Winckelmann" Pater expands his definition of humanism, making it also the spur of creativity:

> The basis of all artistic genius lies in the power of conceiving humanity in a new and striking way,

of putting a happy world of its own creation in place of the meaner world of our common days, generating around itself an atmosphere with a novel power of refraction, selecting, transforming, recombining the images it transmits, according to the choice of the imaginative intellect.[35]

From this rendition of the origins of the artistic process, it is but a short step to the qualities which similarly serve to give some unity to life:

> A taste for metaphysics may be one of those things which we must renounce, if we mean to mould our lives to artistic perfection. Philosophy serves culture, not by the fancied gift of absolute or transcendental knowledge, but by suggesting questions which help one to detect the passion, and strangeness, and dramatic contrasts of life.[36]

The example of Winckelmann comes to us seemingly imperfect because we can perceive no final and decisive solution to the problem of transiency except in a transforming vision that may, for a moment, unify experience. Winckelmann does, however, stand as the exemplar of a *modus vivendi;* as with Wordsworth, Winckelmann's approach to life and to art is one of "impassioned contemplation." This Pater considers "the end-in-itself, the perfect end." Attaining this end—the goal of Winckelmann's life and of Wordsworth's—becomes a "higher morality," a sort of late Victorian existentialism.

> That the end of life is not action but contemplation—*being* as distinct from *doing*—a certain disposition of the mind: is, in some shape or other, the principle of all the higher morality. In poetry, in art, if you enter into their true spirit at all, you

touch this principle, in a measure: these, by their very sterility, are a type of beholding for the mere joy of beholding. To treat life in the spirit of art, is to make life a thing in which means and ends are identified: to encourage such treatment, the true moral significance of art and poetry. Wordsworth, and other poets who have been like him in ancient or more recent times, are the masters, the experts, in this art of impassioned contemplation. Their work is, not to teach lessons, or enforce rules, or even to stimulate us to noble ends; but to withdraw the thoughts for a little while from the mere machinery of life, to fix them, with appropriate emotions, on the spectacle of those great facts in man's existence which no machinery affects, "on the great and universal passions of men, the most general and interesting of their occupations, and the entire world of nature,"—on "the operations of the elements and the appearances of the visible universe, on storm and sunshine, on the revolutions of the seasons, on cold and heat, on loss of friends and kindred, on injuries and resentments, on gratitude and hope, on fear and sorrow." To witness this spectacle with appropriate emotions is the aim of all culture; and of these emotions poetry like Wordsworth's is a great nourisher and stimulant. He sees nature full of sentiment and excitement; he sees men and women as parts of nature, passionate, excited, in strange grouping and connexion with the grandeur and beauty of the natural world:—images, in his own words, "of man suffering, amid awful forms and powers."[37]

Part of Wordsworth's ability to attain some degree of "impassioned contemplation" derives from his humanistic ability to respond to the train of experience beyond his local setting. Like Winckelmann, Wordsworth exercises his contemplation for purposes of revitalizing and recombining.

> Thinking of the high value he set upon customariness, upon all that is habitual, local, rooted in the ground, in matters of religious sentiment, you might sometimes regard him as one tethered down to a world, refined and peaceful indeed, but with no broad outlook, a world protected, but somewhat narrowed, by the influence of received ideas. But he is at times also something very different from this, and something much bolder. A chance expression is overheard and placed in a new connexion, the sudden memory of a thing long past occurs to him, a distant object is relieved for a while by a random gleam of light—accidents turning up for a moment what lies below the surface of our immediate experience—and he passes from the humble graves and lowly arches of "the little rock-like pile" of a Westmoreland church, on bold trains of speculative thought, and comes, from point to point, into strange contact with thoughts which have visited, from time to time, far more venturesome, perhaps errant, spirits.[38]

Although Wordsworth's contemplation results in a sensing of a Platonic preexistence, his mode of thought is hardly different from that of Winckelmann, for whom Greece was like another home from which he was separated by circumstances and accident. And Winckelmann's life as the ideal looms before us:

> In Winckelmann, this [type of Greek art] comes to him [Goethe], not as in a book or a theory, but more importunately, because in a passionate life, in a personality.[39]

Pater points towards a mode of thought about life which offers modern man in his separation from "completeness, centrality" the best alternative to living in the edenic time-before. *The Renaissance, Appreciations, Greek Studies,* and *Plato and Platonism* represent Pater's contributions to the literature about the House Beautiful, just as *Marius, Imaginary Portraits,* and *Gaston de Latour* represent his contributions to the structure itself. But the edifice of created things, independent of Pater's contribution, and the flow of life which continually adds new artifacts to the edifice exist for the willing apprehender as the means of solace. With an intense enough projection, the self may arrest its own transiency, at least for a moment, and identify with the edifice it beholds.

CHAPTER THREE

The Living & the Dead

He heard the snow falling faintly through the universe and faintly falling, like the descent of their last end, upon all the living and the dead.

James Joyce, "The Dead"

T HE SNOW THAT falls outside Gabriel Conroy's window in Joyce's "The Dead" serves several purposes. It provides a setting for the action at the end of the story. It insolates Conroy and his wife to some extent from the world around them. And it brings to Conroy's mind the image of Michael Furey, who had, at another time and another place, died into the snow and whose renewed existence depends on the snow. When Conroy swoons, he is aware of little but the snow and the image of Michael Furey. The swoon, itself a medial state between life and death, brings Conroy paradoxically to his most intense awareness of himself and of his future course in life.

Like art and experience, the snow links the living and the dead. One reading of "The Dead" suggests the equivalence of snow and what Richard Ellmann calls "mutuality."[1] Like the snow in Joyce's story, art and experience body forth the image, in this case the image of Michael Furey. And the apprehension of that image, like Gabriel Conroy's of the Irish poet with the dark, expressive eyes, effects a change in the perceiver. The "journey westward" is a journey to primitive origins and also a journey to death—a death that will bring Conroy closer to Michael Furey than he had ever thought he could be. The swoon, the "identity . . . fading out into a grey impalpable world," represents the resultant merging of the consciousness of the perceiver with the consciousness bodied forth in the artistic or snow-born image.

> A few light taps upon the pane made him turn
> to the window. It had begun to snow again. He

watched sleepily the flakes, silver and dark, falling obliquely against the lamplight. The time had
come for him to set out on his journey westward.
Yes, the newspapers were right: snow was general
all over Ireland. It was falling on every part of
the dark central plain, on the treeless hills, falling
softly upon the Bog of Allen and, farther westward,
softly falling into the dark mutinous Shannon
waves. It was falling, too, upon every part of the
lonely churchyard on the hill where Michael Furey
lay buried. It lay thickly drifted on the crooked
crosses and headstones, on the spears of the little
gate, on the barren thorns. His soul swooned slowly
as he heard the snow falling faintly through the
universe and faintly falling, like the descent of
their last end, upon all the living and the dead.[2]

The ending of "The Dead" represents one of the
fullest realizations of Pater's esthetic, and the use of
the esthetic by a writer of Joyce's stature testifies to
the effect of Pater on the writers of his own time and
the succeeding generation. The Pater delivered to us
by Joyce may seem more satisfactory than the Pater of
Marius the Epicurean or *The Renaissance*. But Pater's
own writings show a conscious movement towards what
proves to be the ideal realization by Joyce, and at its
best Pater's own fiction repays a close reading. In "The
Dead" Joyce plays down the effect of the immediate
physical image, in this case of Michael Furey, while
Pater delivers it to us for what it may be worth in
itself, which in context is a great deal. Ideally Pater
attempts to please esthetically by showing the physical,
as well as to teach something about the nature of art.
Practically, however, Pater serves best as a directive to
our thinking about the nature of art, and about the
relationship of art to life. If Pater's vivid descriptions

of physical beauty sometimes border on the perverse, they nonetheless demonstrate the importance of the human image in art. For Pater, the full realization of the human image in prose is a necessary part of his humanism. In art, as in life, the human image demands a response from the apprehender.

The most difficult thing to achieve in reading Pater is the appropriate degree of "impassioned contemplation," the mode of response Pater suggests in the "Conclusion" to *The Renaissance*. To some extent, the problem is one of preconceptions: the idea that Pater is an "impressionist" critic interferes.[3] (Pater calls himself an "impressionist" critic; he does imply that he is an "aesthetic critic," the critic in "The School of Giorgione" that he considers the ideal.) Pater's impressionism, in both his criticism and his fiction, bears redefining. "Impressionism" is, after all, an over-easy and imprecise term, and insofar as it is applied to Pater it has unfortunate connotations of superficiality and facility. Pater does try to give his reader an impression. But more important, he tries to communicate a physical sensation through prose. Whether the sensation be one welling up from the imagination, from the life around him, or from works of art matters little to Pater. The intensely physical image conceived by Pater works to impress itself on the reader's mind, drawing from him a response which involves the emotions as well as the more narrowly defined appreciation of pure form.

In his essay on Winckelmann, Pater describes what he calls the "pagan manner" of dealing with the sensuous in art:

> A serenity—*Heiterkeit*— . . . characterizes Winckelmann's handling of the sensuous side of Greek art. This serenity is, perhaps, in great measure, a

73

> negative quality: it is the absence of any sense
> of want, or corruption, or shame. With the sen-
> suous element in Greek art he deals in the pagan
> manner; . . . the artist steeps his thought again
> and again into the fire of colour. To the Greek
> this immersion in the sensuous was, religiously,
> at least, indifferent. Greek sensuousness, there-
> fore, does not fever the conscience: it is shameless
> and childlike. . . . [Winckelmann] fingers those
> pagan marbles with unsinged hands, with no sense
> of shame or loss. That is to deal with the sensuous
> side of art in the pagan manner.[4]

Winckelmann's response to Greek statues is analogous
to the reader's response to Pater's prose: Pater presents
the physical with a frank sensuousness in which he
expects his reader to delight. The result, presumably,
is "impassioned contemplation," something like the
famous "tactile response" described by Bernard Berenson, an early follower of Pater. To what extent the
response is erotic is a moot point.

Art, for Pater, is humanistic partly because of its
focus on the human image. The constant element in
art is man. The artist works with the human image to
make it recall to the apprehender the whole range of
ideas, of experiences which the image embodies. And
as common factor in both life and art, the human image
serves as the point of connection. The apprehender
responds to the human image in art much as he might
respond to the human image in life, albeit frequently
with expanded associations. Gabriel Conroy's perception of Michael Furey in "The Dead" leads him to a
new appreciation of the living and of the complex relationship between living and dead. As Conroy's swoon
suggests, the line of demarcation is a vague one indeed;
yet the result of Conroy's vision will probably be a

fuller appreciation of his wife's place in his life, of her needs. Much of the change depends on the influence of the dead Michael Furey. For a moment, Michael Furey is very real to Conroy, for art, like the snow in "The Dead," offers the human image to the apprehender much as the apprehender might receive it in life.

In *Plato and Platonism,* Pater discusses the relation of the human image to the flow of ideas.[5] As with Pico della Mirandola in *The Renaissance,* one senses Pater's identification with his subject in his warm approval. Pater attributes Plato's continuing popularity to the "impress of visible reality" which runs through his work.[6] Visible reality dominates Pater's work too: as critic Pater centers his efforts on the visual arts and as creator he endeavors to give a strong visual impression of his characters.[7]

With Pater as with Plato, also, the sum of ideas expresses itself through the image of a person. Pater's description of Plato's sensuous and "humanistic" approach to his material serves as a description of his own approach as well.

> Now Plato is one for whom the visible world thus "really exists" because he is by nature and before all things, from first to last, unalterably a lover. In that, precisely, lies the secret of the susceptible and diligent eye, the so sensitive ear. The central interest of his own youth—of his profoundly impressible youth—as happens always with natures of real capacity, gives law and pattern to all that succeeds it. Τὰ ἐρωτικά, as he says, the experience, the discipline, of love, had been that for Plato; and, as love must of necessity deal above all with visible persons, this discipline involved an exquisite culture of the senses. It is "as lovers use," that he is ever on the watch for those dainty messages,

those finer intimations, to eye and ear. If in the later development of his philosophy the highest sort of knowledge comes to seem like the knowledge of a person, the relation of the reason to truth like the commerce of one person with another, the peculiarities of personal relationship thus moulding his conception of the properly invisible world of ideas, this is partly because, for a lover, the entire visible world, its hues and outline, its attractiveness, its power and bloom, must have associated themselves pre-eminently with the power and bloom of visible living persons. With these, as they made themselves known by word and glance and touch, through the medium of the senses, lay the forces, which, in that inexplicable tyranny of one person over another, shaped the soul.[8]

The emphasis Pater places on Plato's attention to the physical world surprises the reader who might expect the conventional metaphysically-minded philosopher. But with Pater the mind always moves from the specific physical object to the metaphysical speculation which the object may bring forth. Gerald Monsman makes the point in his *Pater's Portraits:* "Pater seems to be giving us here, in the single figure projected against the background of humanity, his equivalent to those delicate Greek coins stamped with the profile of Demeter—'an epitome of art on a larger scale' (*Greek Studies*, p. 138), as he remarks."[9] This preoccupation with the physically specific supersedes any interest on Pater's part in the metaphysical or the abstruse. Since the emphasis is on the physical, the metaphysical intrudes only sparingly. Physical beauty, such as the physical form of the liturgy of the early church in *Marius the Epicurean*, may lead Pater to a position of sympathy for the metaphysical idea growing out of the apprehended phenomena. But as in Pater's Plato, the commitment to any one metaphysical position is at best fleeting; the firmer and prior commitment is to the physical image.

The physical image to which Pater most often directs the reader's response is, of course, the human form—either issuing forth from Pater's imagination or as interpreted by Pater in a work of art. Thus the esthetic quality and the physical beauty become one and the same, reinforcing each other and becoming indistinct from each other. Pater's description of the *Venus of Melos* typifies his own intentions in physical description and bears reexamination.

> But take a work of Greek art,—the Venus of Melos. That is in no sense a symbol, a suggestion, of anything beyond its own victorious fairness. The mind begins and ends with the finite image, yet loses no part of the spiritual motive. That motive is not lightly and loosely attached to the sensuous form, as its meaning to an allegory, but saturates and is identical with it. The Greek mind had advanced to a particular stage of self-reflexion, but was careful not to pass beyond it. . . . In Greek thought . . . the "lordship of the soul" is recognized; that lordship gives authority and divinity to human eyes and hands and feet; inanimate nature is thrown into the background. But just there Greek thought finds its happy limit; it has not yet become too inward; the mind has not yet learned to boast its independence of the flesh.[10]

The passage in the essay on Winckelmann exhibits a number of themes that recur in Pater's prose: a distrust of the metaphysical (Greek thought is not yet "too inward"); an assertion of the interpenetration of form and matter (the spiritual motive is one with the physical image); and—most important of all—the communication of an overriding sense of physical beauty. The statue's "victorious fairness" impresses itself on the mind and becomes the embodiment of any projected thinking "beyond itself."

Pater's preoccupation with sensuous beauty manifests itself in his life as well as in his writings. Thomas Wright records a characteristic anecdote:

> Another "coquetry" of his room—to use his own expression—was a bust of Hercules (and we have already referred to the admiration by the weakling Pater for men of muscle and sinew). "Hercules, Discobolus, Samson, these"—exclaimed one of Pater's admirers—"these be thy gods, O Pater." Beside an oval representing Venus, Cupid and the eagle of Jupiter in mid-air hung prints of "Paris awarding the apple" and "The Toilette of Venus." . . . Join to this information that he had for servant one Harry Charlwood—a good-looking man of middle-height, with dark whiskers and a fresh complexion—and one gets a very fair idea of Pater and his surroundings at the time he entered Brasenose.[11]

Wright, whose ability to collect suggestive anecdotes was surpassed only by his willingness to ignore their implications, gives a satisfactory description of Pater's demand for comeliness in the world about him:

> If lack of good looks in himself troubled Pater, he was also troubled by plainness in others. If a man was ugly he avoided his society. All his friends were good-looking. Plainness appealed not to him,

no matter how clever it might be. All ugly objects were painful to him. Even Goethe did not pass butchers' shops more rapidly.[12]

One might cite Pater's fondness for the costumed splendor of religious ceremony, for beautifully bound volumes, for good architecture. Usually one approaches Pater to get through his prose the impression he offers of these things. The effect, however, is often much more than an impression. Pater gives us what amounts to a verbal reconstruction of the thing being described. The human form is his favorite subject.

Like most romantics, especially Keats, Pater devotes much thought to the transiency of the self, particularly insofar as the self is identical with and subject to the changes of the physical form that embodies it. Thus the spiritual motive—the "victorious fairness" of the form and the embodied self—gains its preservation through the preservation of the form in art. In Pater's esthetic, the artist preserves the spiritual motive by giving a close description of the form which embodies it. The "higher morality" of which Pater speaks in his essay on Wordsworth[13] indicates how the problem is approached in life: the perceiver attempts to be at one with the perceived, thus arresting his own transiency and becoming part of the perfect form which he beholds. The artist who puts the human form into his work of art similarly delivers man into art; so transiency is arrested in the physical sense by the transformation of the human into the human image. In either case, the work of art is a stay against time: the apprehender momentarily goes outside himself to become part of the perfect form, or the ephemeral human form is transformed by the creator and as human image becomes part of a timeless perfect form. In one case the motivating power is the beholder's "desire of beauty"; in the other, it is the artist's transforming power. The romantic version of this conventional esthetic, as it manifests itself in Pater, directs the artist's attention to the human image as the form most worthy of preservation. Pater's repeated choice of the human form in death as his image fits with his Romantic esthetic; death may be considered that "quality of strangeness" added to beauty which for Pater defined romanticism.

For Pater, the human form becomes an artistic object, an artifact, similar to Poe's lovely embalmed women or to Oscar Wilde's Dorian Gray. Wilde's novel reverses Pater's premise. Gray's body stays young and his portrait grows old. Yet Wilde opts for Pater's principle in the end when Gray dies and the picture regains its lost beauty. The presentation of the human form in the visual arts demands, in every period, a corresponding presentation in literature. Sir Joshua Reynolds recognizes the fact in his *Discourses,* which are, in the strict sense, an academic attempt to find for the painter a prescriptive verbal equivalent for the human form, just as painting and sculpture attempt to find a visual and sometimes a tactile equivalent. Reynolds writes a handbook for the artist; Pater attempts to communicate directly a sensuous experience, his apprehension of the form, whether in life or in art or in imagination. The complex and not strictly limited medium of prose seems for Pater the proper vehicle for conveying sensual delight. Symons analyzes the peculiar competence with which Pater manipulated his medium to accomplish his ends:

> Pater seemed to draw up into himself every form
> of earthly beauty, or of the beauty made by men,

. . . and a sense of human things which was neither that of the lover nor of the priest, but partly of both; and his work was the giving out of this again, with a certain labor to give it wholly.[14]

For Symons, the "giving out again" of beauty already apprehended by the imagination or the senses forms the core of Pater's work. Symons means, of course, that Pater is an artist. Most often the beauty Pater gives out, however, is the beauty of man in his "victorious fairness." In *Marius,* for example, Pater leads the reader to respond favorably to the first appearance of Flavian.

He [Marius] had seen Flavian for the first time the day on which he had come to Pisa, at the moment when his mind was full of wistful thoughts regarding the new life to begin for him tomorrow, and he gazed curiously at the crowd of bustling scholars as they came from their classes. There was something in Flavian a shade disdainful, as he stood isolated from the others for a moment, explained in part by his stature and the distinction of the low, broad forehead; though there was pleasantness also for the newcomer in the roving blue eyes which seemed somehow to take a fuller hold upon things around than is usual with boys. Marius knew that those proud glances made kindly note of him for a moment, and felt something like friendship at first sight. There was a tone of reserve or gravity there, amid perfectly disciplined health, which, to his fancy, seemed to carry forward the expression of the austere sky and the clear song of the blackbird on that gray March evening. Flavian indeed was a creature who changed much with the changes of the passing light and shade about him, and was brilliant enough under the early sunshine in school next morning. Of all that little world of more or

less gifted youth, surely the centre was this lad of
servile birth. Prince of the school, he had gained
an easy dominion over the old Greek master by
the fascination of his parts, and over his fellow-
scholars by the figure he bore. He wore already the
manly dress; and standing there in class, as he
displayed his wonderful quickness in reckoning, or
his taste in declaiming Homer, he was like a carved
figure in motion, thought Marius, but with that
indescribable gleam upon it which the words of
Homer actually suggested, as perceptible on the
visible forms of the gods—οἶα θεοὺς ἐπενήνοθεν αἰὲν
ἐόντας.[15]

Pater manipulates the point of view and directs the
attention to detail so that the reader first appreciates
Flavian solely as a virile, physical being and only later
as a character with interesting intellectual qualities.

As in much of the novel, the reader sees from Marius's
point of view. The "wistful thoughts" of Marius regarding his new life may be the "thoughts of a limit to
duration, of inevitable decay, of dispossession" which
trouble most of Pater's favorite characters. As elsewhere, however, the ideal physical beauty that takes
sensual possession of the mind momentarily drives out
the thought of decay and restores, however briefly,
wholeness and joy. Pater directs the reader to Flavian's
isolation as a beautiful verbal artifact. Flavian seems
almost a carved figure. Not only does he stand out
from the crowd "disdainful," but also he emerges as a
kind of physical symbol of wholeness amid a turgid
swim of philosophical speculation. The realization of
Flavian takes an increasingly sensual tone as the passage
progresses. The impression of disdain gains the reader's
favor, especially when he finds that the other youths—

all anonymous—are only "more or less gifted." The reader, like Marius a "newcomer," senses the "pleasantness . . . in the roving blue eyes" which possess what they fall on more "than is usual." And the pleasantness modifies the disdain, especially when the eyes make "kindly note" of Marius. The "perfectly disciplined health" dispels the earlier wistful thoughts. Needless to say, Pater intends Flavian to take as complete a hold on the reader as he does on Marius. Flavian becomes protean: changing with "the passing light and shade about him," but maintaining his initial sensual appeal as a beautiful image. Physical perfection becomes characterization. Flavian demands "something like friendship at first sight."

The response resembles that described in the fragment "An English Poet," apparently originally intended as one of the first series of *Imaginary Portraits*. The poet, still a young man, awaits a friend on the coast of France. As he waits, he experiences a variety of physical stimuli which work upon his senses and evoke the image of his friend:

> The sparkling light and lovely colours here in the brilliant air blent themselves to a unity very soothing to one's animal spirits. The mere physical exhilaration which came with those smooth winds from the sea, the overwrought sensibility with which he seemed to appreciate the material elements as it were of their balm and salt, coaxing him into a sort of renewed life, might . . . have been the sign of the action already within him of that strange malady . . . and which was established in him by that long tension of spirit to which the distinction of his intellectual quality was due. . . . so it was that above all intellectual or poetic

enjoyment of the novelties around him there pre-
ponderated a wholly physical satisfaction in the
quickening impulse of the air, the breath of the
sea and salt, weeds in blossom or turning to
decay. . . .

. . . The variety and expansiveness of the peculiar
scene witnessed thus for the first time in mature
manhood seemed to unseal his sense of the actual
life of men as passionate or graceful. Fancies,
divinations of a real experience as a thing that
might be refulgent with ideal light and satisfy a
poetic soul, germinating rapidly in him a warmth,
a *souffle,* almost like love towards the friend who
was coming, came to him, as the strong air from
the waves and the scent of the beanfield met about
him.[16]

The fragment represents something of a prose attempt at the meditative-reflective poem, albeit given in
the third person. One thinks of Coleridge's "The
Aeolian Harp" and even of "Frost at Midnight." The
natural setting works on the poet's sensibility and
brings him broadened human sympathy. The Cole-
ridgean beanfield is only one of several examples of
Pater's debt to the poetic form. Pater left "An English
Poet" both unfinished and unpublished. It is thus
valuable as a revelation of the workings of his mind at
some point earlier than that arrived at in the finished
product. The influence of the physical stimuli upon
the mind of the young poet, like the influence of
Flavian's appearance upon Marius, leads to love. Pater's
more sensuous passages those on the *Mona Lisa* and
the *Birth of Venus,* for example, come close to erotic
fantasy, and the young poet's vision seems in danger

of approaching voyeurism. Possibly his closeness to fantasy in "An English Poet" caused him to leave the portrait unfinished. (Pater concluded with the second passage quoted above.) The image of beauty as the mind apprehends it draws the requisite sympathetic response. Pater evokes the friend of the young poet through the description of landscape detail; the image of Flavian presents itself to the reader more directly as artifact. "Beauty becomes a distinction," with the lowborn Flavian, "like genius, or noble place."[17]

The detailed physical description in "Emerald Uthwart," an Imaginary Portrait which appears in *Miscellaneous Studies,* aims at getting from the reader a reaction to physical beauty similar to that the reader gets from *Marius.* The effort is less skillful, if more explicit.

> But only see him [Uthwart] as he goes. It is as if he left music, delightfully throbbing music, or flowers, behind him, as he passes. . . . Strangers' eyes, resting on him by chance, are deterred for a while . . . [he] goes in . . . like youth's very self, eternal, immemorial, eternally renewed, about those immemorially ancient stones. "Young Apollo!" people say—people who have pigeon-holes for their impressions, watching the slim, trim figure with the exercise books. His very dress seems touched with Hellenic fitness to the healthy youthful form. "Golden-haired, scholar Apollo!" they repeat, foolishly, ignorantly. He was better; was more like a real portrait of a real young Greek, like *Tryphon, Son of Eutychos,* for instance (as friends remembered him with regret, as you may see him still on his tombstone in the British Museum), alive among the paler physical and

intellectual lights of modern England. . . . The
theatrical old Greek god never took the expressive-
ness, the lines of delicate meaning, such as were
come into the face of the English lad, the phys-
iognomy of his race; ennobled now, as if by the
writing, the signature, there, of a grave intelligence,
by grave information and a subdued will, though
without a touch of melancholy in this "best of play-
fellows." . . . The somewhat unmeaningly handsome facial type of the Uthwarts, moulded to a
mere animal or physical perfection through whole-
some centuries, is breathed on now, informed, by
the touches, traces, complex influences from past
and present a thousandfold, crossing each other in
this late century, and yet at unity in the simple
law of the system to which he is now subject.[18]

The youthful image attains its archetypal integrity not
so much by the conventional analogies with music or
flowers as by the extended and evocative physical
description. The clothes through which the form is
revealed remind the reader of the drapery of painting
or sculpture, beneath which the physical tension asserts
itself, with the beholder's interest increased by the
concealment. And like the *Mona Lisa,* the face exhibits
a delicate impress of varied suggestiveness. Pater never
becomes completely explicit in his descriptions, for the
reader must participate in the imaginative creation of
the form—as with Flavian in the changing light. Yet
his implications are explicit enough so the reader can
hardly avoid the sensual response.[19]

Marius's "wistfulness," the sometime Greek "thoughts
of a limit to duration" are the problem which life
presents to art for a solution. The embodiment of the
physical in prose is one way in which the human form

achieves permanence. The physical description, however, has implications beyond its realization of the
human form as verbal artifact. Pater commits himself
to giving life to the form, recognizing, like all romantics,
that to do so he must show it in death as inviolate.

Pater's most specific treatment of the human form
in death comes in "The Age of Athletic Prizemen," the
concluding section of *Greek Studies*.[20] The essay considers a phase of Greek sculpture, and the argument
develops, like most of Pater's arguments, as a discussion
of the relationship of art to life, the discussion using
the works of art under scrutiny as a body of materials
from which Pater can extrapolate the desired conclu-
sions. Pater begins by noting that medieval art sometimes reminds the viewer of Greek art and that Greek
art sometimes reminds the viewer of medieval art.

Some critics lament Pater's tendency to find dichot-
omies where none exist.[21] Pater goes for the dichotomy
as the mouse for the cheese. But his efforts differ little
from those of any other romantic; they are simply more
overt, partly, no doubt, because Pater's romantic tendencies sometimes conflict with his appreciation of the
classical. Or, more correctly, Pater's romanticism colors
his appreciation of the classical.

Thus the reading of the statue of Venus becomes a
romantic response to the classical world, along the
lines suggested in the "Postscript" to *Appreciations*.
Pater does, however, frequently achieve the fusion of
opposites for which he works, even if only descriptively.[22]
One must remember that Pater's theory of history—a
theory which Yeats follows in this instance—begins with
classicism and follows with Christianity, then with
Christianity as modified by the reintroduction of classicism, and ends with the relativistic spirit of modernity.

The attempt at fusion of opposites appealed to Pater both because of his classical inclinations and because of his origins in the romantic movement. The "Postscript" to *Appreciations* draws classic and romantic closer together. His linking of the medieval and the Greek modes depends on his definition of humanism as the belief that whatever moved men once can never wholly lose its vitality. The second dichotomy of the essay, however, contributes more to an understanding of his resolution of the contraries of the living and the dead.

The Greeks, he notes, "cared much always for the graves of the dead." Even the young desired "a *frequented* tomb." Pater describes the "Harpy tomb" from Xanthus, now in the British Museum, and the scene depicted on the tomb serves as the basis for Pater's discussion of the paradox:

> A cow . . . is one of almost any number of artistic symbols of new-birth, of the renewal of life, drawn from a world which is, after all, so full of it. On one side sits enthroned, as some have thought, the Goddess of Death; on the opposite side the Goddess of Life, with her flowers and fruit. Towards her three young maidens are advancing —were they still alive thus, graceful, virginal, with their long, plaited hair, and long, delicately-folded tunics, looking forward to carry on their race into the future? Presented severally, on the other sides of the dark hollow within, three male persons—a young man, an old man, and a boy—seem to be bringing home, somewhat wearily, to their "long home," the young man, his armour, the boy, and the old man, like old Socrates, the mortuary cock, as they approach some shadowy ancient diety of the tomb.[23]

The icons of birth and death are interesting in their number, but most interesting is the conception of the young girls carrying their race, both artistically and physically, into the future. A subsequent passage describes the similarly paradoxical return of the warrior-boy from his tomb to the world of the living:

> The surviving thought of the lad Trypho, returning from his tomb to the living, was of athletic character; how he was and looked when in the flower of his strength. And it is not of the dead but of the living, who look and are as he, that the artistic genius of this period is full.[24]

For Pater the fact of the image of life on the tomb is the Greek resolution of the paradox of life in death. The tomb image commemorates death but is of life; it is "full" of the living.

The Greek realization of continuing life in the image of death, as in the figure on the tomb, gave Pater half the answer to the paradox. For Pater, continuing life meant, as it had for the Greeks, continuing physical beauty. Thus the beauty of the corpse in "Emerald Uthwart":

> Deceased was his twenty-seventh year, but looked many years younger; had indeed scarcely yet reached the full condition of manhood. The extreme purity of the outlines, both of the face and limbs, was such as is usually found only in quite early youth; the brow especially, under an abundance of fair hair, finely formed, not high, but arched and full, as is said to be the way with those who have the imaginative temper in excess. . . . I was struck by the great beauty of the organic developments, in the strictly anatomic sense; those

of the throat and diaphragm in particular might have been modelled for a teacher of normal physiology, or a professor of design. The flesh was still almost as firm as that of a living person; as happens when, as in this case, death comes to all intents and purposes as gradually as in old age. The expression of health and life . . . touched me to a degree very unusual. . . . The ball . . . was at length removed. . . . The flowers were then hastily replaced, the hands and the peak of the handsome nose remaining visible among them; the wind ruffled the fair hair a little; the lips were still red. I shall not forget it.[25]

Pater does allow himself the device of a "Surgeon's Report" as a vehicle for the description. But the tone resembles that of the earlier depiction of the young Uthwart. The emphasis on youth, the extraordinary preservation of the body, even the wind-ruffled hair give an appealing quality to the physical image. The passage just evades suggesting necrophilia because of the emphasis on life: the body is without life only in its stillness and even the stillness is relieved by the action of the wind as it ruffles the hair.

In his other descriptions, too, Pater gives some hint of anticipated death. Flavian's gravity in his first appearance only faintly suggests the end to which he will come. The body of Flavian is cremated, the cremation obviates the necessity of dealing with the decay of the physical image. Certainly Pater chose a proper pagan expedient as his answer to the problem of how to get the artifact out of the story without having it decay. In "Emerald Uthwart" the story ends before the form can degenerate, and the physical image remains for the reader in its full integrity, though almost motionless.

The Greeks, though, contributed further to the resolution of the problem which Pater adapted for his artistic purposes. "An Age of Athletic Prizemen" describes the forms the body took in Greek sculpture:

> Now, this predominance of youth, of the youthful form, in art, of bodily gymnastic promoting natural advantages to the utmost, of the physical perfection developed thereby, is a sign that essential mastery has been achieved by the artist—the power, that is to say, of a full and free realization. For such youth, in its very essence, is a matter properly within the limits of the visible, the empirical, world. . . . In any passable representation of the Greek *discobolus,* as in any passable representation of an English cricketer, there can be no successful evasion of the natural difficulties of the thing to be done—the difficulties of competing with nature itself, or its maker, in that marvellous combination of motion and rest, of inward mechanism with the so smoothly finished surface and outline —finished *ad unguem*—which enfold it.[26]

Two variations in the realization of physical form dominate:

> Those works are reducible to two famous original types—the *Discobolus* or quoit-player of Myron, the *beau idéal* (we may use that term for once justly) of athletic motion; and the *Diadumenus* of Polycleitus, as, binding the fillet or crown of victory upon his head, he presents the *beau idéal* of athletic repose, and almost begins to think.[27]

And the reconciliation of the two types is in the *Discobolus at Rest* at the Vatican.

> We might accept him for that *canon,* or measure, of the perfect human form, which Polycleitus has

proposed. He is neither the victor at rest, as with Polycleitus, nor the combatant already in motion, as with Myron, but, as if stepping backward from Myron's precise point of interest, he is preparing for his venture, taking stand carefully on the right foot. Eye and mind concentre, loyally, entirely, upon the business in hand. . . . Take him to lead you forth quite out of the narrow limits of the Greek world.[28]

Because the figure is about to go into motion, he represents the perfect resolution of rest and motion. As such, he can attain no further perfection in the Greek world and will lead to a new perfection (or search for it) in a post-Greek world. The Greek world can attain no more and must give way. The resolution of repose and motion for the sculptor lies in combination. Pater extends the sculptural analogy into his prose and uses it as part of his solution to the problem of giving the human artifact death so that it may have life.

Repose, as in the case of Emerald Uthwart, is for Pater sometimes the only indication of death. There is an obvious analogy between repose (particularly when it takes the form of sleep) and death, between motion and life. The achievement of resolved motion and repose becomes for Pater, as for the Greeks, an artistic ideal. In his essay on Winckelmann, Pater attempts to characterize the ideal:

In the best Greek sculpture, the archaic immobility has been stirred, its forms are in motion; but it is a motion ever kept in reserve, and very seldom committed to any definite action.[29]

The passage recalls the beauty of the dead Emerald Uthwart, his hair moved slightly by the wind. And thus also the living Flavian, who in his realization as verbal artifact is paradoxically "like a carved figure in motion." The potential for motion likewise manifests itself in the *Mona Lisa*. The holy voluptuary resembles the vampire and "has been dead many times"; but she is still a "diver in deep seas." In her combination of qualities she, like Pater's other verbal realizations of human form, has a quality of "perpetual life." Her continued existence as verbal artifact, which can hardly be questioned, depends upon the skillful balance of death and life, repose and motion.

Pater's own most thoroughgoing and consistent realization of his humanist esthetic comes in a tale where the insistence upon the physical bows to the larger realization of its artistic implications. "Duke Carl of Rosenmold," the fourth of the *Imaginary Portraits*,[30] resembles Wilde's fairy tales, and the fantasy works effectively both to sublimate the physical motive in Pater's art and to serve as a fictional demonstration of his esthetic. The tale has the additional merits of showing Pater successfully handling a structure based upon narrative development rather than on repeated verbal motifs and of being a delightful, if bittersweet, epitome of the fanciful tale.

The portrait presents the young Duke Carl as something of an ideal esthete. The young heir to a small German principality, he decides to bring the trappings of art to his state and so imports numerous French plays and French looking glasses for his own and his people's enjoyment. The Duke's affectation of the French mode tends to the ridiculous, but only pleasantly so. Tiring of his unsatisfying esthetic endeavor, the heir tries to make art of his own life by counterfeiting his own death. Clad as a minstrel he follows his own funeral procession, ministers to a poor common woman who had admired him, and shortly thereafter reappears as the slightly mad Carl, returning to life. The heir Carl (referred to throughout as Duke Carl) becomes ruler in his own right after the old Duke dies, but his relationship with his people remains that of one who is half-dead. Duke Carl travels much in Germany and spends little time in his duchy. He returns to Rosenmold to wed a young commoner he had seen when a minstrel. As the wedding is held, marauding soldiers enter the kingdom, and the soldiers possess the kingdom at the moment Duke Carl consummates his marriage. Years later the bones of the Duke and his bride, their rings still on their fingers, burst forth from the ground as an uprooted tree falls in the wind. The narrator of the story relates that he has seen Duke Carl, so he thinks, many years later, walking on the bridge in his city.

Pater skillfully begins the tale with the discovery of the bones in a "stormy season." The question is posed whether the bones were buried on purpose beneath the tree, the answer being that they probably were not. Yet the bones fulfill the popular expectation of "buried treasure" to be found beneath the soil. The analogy of the bones to treasure is borne out by the "rich golden ornaments" found about the remains. The "long-remembering people" know the bones to be those of Duke Carl. Since the bones are the motive for the tale—the narrator must tell the tale of Duke Carl after their discovery—the relationship of the physical form to art (as a spur to creation) is established. The discovery of the bones represents also, however, the physical form as preserved in nature (the physical form is one of several analogical forms of art in the tale) and the bursting forth from the roots of the fallen tree indicates the reappearance of the human image or artifact in each generation. Goethe, for example, represents a more perfect realization of what Duke Carl tries to do for Germany. (The further implication is that the image—in this case the human image—gives birth to new forms of the image, that is, the possibly modified telling of the tale of Duke Carl by the narrator.) The "long-remembering people" are those who apprehend the continuity of the human image in each reappearance —Pater's humanists. That time has seemed to stand still for ages at the court of Rosenmold supports the conclusion that Rosenmold itself stands at certain points in the story as an analogue to art.

People Pater calls *"quasi* decorative" inhabit the image-filled world of Rosenmold—court musicians and poets and the like. These and the artifacts about him, notably a volume by Conrad Celtes with Durer-like illustration, tend to make of young Duke Carl's life one continual ceremony. That the volume is *Ars Versificandi* suggests the mood: the real is gathered up in comely forms, the most comely being that of the beautiful young Duke himself. The effect is to invest the flux with a kind of permanence, through ceremony. But even the trappings of the state funeral do not appeal to the young man until the ceremony becomes something in which he can be both participant and spectator. When the funeral becomes his own, the Duke attends as minstrel and as supposed corpse. In the funeral the implications of the imported Raphael Madonna become clear: the Duke cannot bring art to his people until he brings it in his own person with himself as artificer and artifact. Raphael's Madonna resembles an "unpretending nun." The Duke as minstrel, however, brings comfort to a woman who has mourned his passing; he comes to her as a new and created personality, the hitherto nonexistent minstrel, but he also comes as full realization of Pater's humanist ideal, that is, in his own person. The Duke becomes one of those "outward and sensuous products of mind" which he himself so admires. (The woman "half" detects him "through his disguise.") The funeral itself represents an attempt by the Duke as artificer to remedy the "threadbare" and "prosaic" quality of daily life in Rosenmold, to justify the seemingly hollow title of "the Apollo of Germany" bestowed upon him by flatterers.

Duke Carl's communion with nature in the south of Germany serves as a further progression of his transformation into artifact. The hold nature takes upon him—telling him "Come! understand, interpret me!"—draws him back to Rosenmold after his journeying and to a better understanding of art. The return and his subsequent marriage represent the final commitment of the self to art; the moment of death and consummation unite, and Duke Carl becomes a part of the natural world, and, by analogy, a part of the world of art. The consummation with the peasant girl indicates the union of the artifact with the apprehender of the artifact (the woman at the funeral, the "long-remembering" people). The death is a birth into art and into new life. The messianic Duke Carl wills himself a kind of immortality that is assured by his dying.

The image is like life but greater, more beautiful than life. The narrator recounts a tale told by Goethe's mother remembering her son: "There, skated my son, like an arrow among the groups. Away he went over the ice like a son of the gods. Anything so beautiful is not to be seen now. I clapped my hands for joy. Never shall I forget him as he darted from one arch of the bridge, and in again under the other, the wind carrying the train behind him as he flew." The narrator sees Goethe as a fulfillment of Duke Carl, the eternal joy of "the aspiring soul of Carl himself,"[31] in freedom and effective at last. The human image moves from art into life, then back into art.

Pater describes his own work accurately in a passage criticizing Morris's poetry:

> One characteristic of the pagan spirit the aesthetic poetry has, which is on its surface—the continual suggestion, pensive or passionate, of the shortness of life. This is contrasted with the bloom of the world, and gives new seduction to it—the sense of death.[32]

Any artistic mode which centers on the shortness of life and the contrasting "bloom of the world" necessarily centers on the human form and its beauty; the memory, collective and individual, of the human form in its particular and general manifestations becomes the artist's problem in art because it is his problem in life. So the young Marius, after the death of Flavian, endeavors by act of will to impress the image of his dead friend upon his consciousness so that it will never be lost.

> The sun shone out on the people going to work for a long hot day, and Marius was standing by the dead, watching, with a deliberate purpose to fix in his memory every detail, that he might have this picture in reserve, should any hour of forget-fulness hereafter come to him with the temptation

to feel completely happy again. A feeling of out-
rage, of resentment against nature itself, mingled
with an agony of pity, as he noted on the now
placid features a certain look of humility, almost
abject, like the expression of a smitten child or
animal, as of one, fallen at last, after bewildering
struggle, wholly under the power of a merciless
adversary. From mere tenderness of soul he would
not forget one circumstance in all that; as a man
might piously stamp on his memory the death-
scene of a brother wrongfully condemned to die,
against a time that may come.[33]

Marius comes to have a fear of the corpse, both because
its decay is the decay of a beautiful image and because
in its decay his own is implicit. The reader may find
his lot easier than Marius's, since he has Flavian's image
in its youthful bloom as well as in its arrested decay.

Marius's complex feelings about the dead and his
connections with them express themselves most explicitly towards the end of the book when he visits the
graves of his ancestors. Marius goes to "the resting
place of his dead" almost sacramentally. His memories
of the place are "burdensome" because he alone carries
them: there is no one else whose memory can give
them "secondary existence."

Dreaming now only of the dead before him, he
journeyed on rapidly through the night; the
thought of them increasing on him, in the dark-
ness. It was as if they had been waiting for him
there through all those years, and felt his footsteps
approaching now, and understood his devotion,
quite gratefully, in that lowliness of theirs, in spite
of its tardy fulfillment. As morning came, his late
tranquillity of mind had given way to a grief which

surprised him by its freshness. He was moved more
than he could have thought possible by so distant a
sorrow. *"To-day!"*—they seemed to be saying as
the hard dawn broke,—*"To-day, he will come!"*
At last, amid all his distractions, they were become
the main purpose of what he was then doing.[34]

When he visits the tomb with an old family servant,
Marius comes to appreciate his father for the first time.
He also comes to understand that it is only in him,
Marius, that the dead he loves have any existence.

> There was a weakness in all this; as there is in
> all care for dead persons, to which nevertheless
> people will always yield in proportion as they
> really care for one another. With a vain yearning,
> as he stood there, still to be able to do something
> for them, he reflected that such doing must be,
> after all, in the nature of things, mainly for himself.
> His own epitaph might be that old one—Ἔσχατος
> τοῦ ἰδίου γένους—*He was the last of his race!*

Because he realizes so intensely that only in himself
do his forbears have any being, Marius has the tombs
covered. Only he can remember them properly; they
are buried "in a way which would claim no sentiment
from the indifferent."[35] Pater is a subtle enough
psychologist to understand that his protagonist's most
generous acts are acts of "self-devotion."

It would be a mistake to ignore the Christian overtones of Marius's visit to the graves of his ancestors.
The incident reminds us of Christ's descent into Hell—
the moment for which the tortured dead have been
waiting and which liberates them. Marius's sacrificial
death, which comes shortly after his visit to the graves,
represents a humanistic re-creation of the crucifixion.

99

The passage in which Marius first beholds the celebration of the eucharist anticipates his own end:

> Marius could discern dimly, behind the solemn
> recitation which now followed, at once a narrative
> and a prayer, the most touching image that had
> ever come within the scope of his mental or physical
> gaze. It was the image of a young man giving up
> voluntarily, one by one, for the greatest of ends,
> the greatest gifts; actually parting with himself,
> above all, with the serenity, the divine serenity, of
> his own soul; yet from the midst of his desolation
> crying out upon the greatness of his success, as if
> foreseeing this very worship.

Pater notes his source as Psalm 22, and the effect is to call attention to the parallels between Christ and David and between Christ and Marius, the three being links in a chain of recurrent types. All of humanity that has gone before seems to become part of the act of worship: "It seemed as if the very dead were aware."[36]

Marius's dead are very much aware that their own joy lies in that of Marius and that their own existence depends on the workings of his sympathetic imagination. Christ releases the tormented from Hell to give them a new grace; Marius confers grace by calling forth in his mind the images of his dead, by giving them the sanctity of being part of the fabric of his memory.

This preservation of the image is for Pater the humanistic ministering of art to the self's awareness of its own transiency. Through memory and through art, the humanist spirit finds realization: "Nothing which has ever interested living men and women can wholly lose its vitality." As humanist, Gabriel Conroy responds to his wife's memory of Michael Furey by apprehending

100

the image in the snow. In his essay on the athletic prizemen, Pater quotes with approval from the Hebrew scriptures, "My delights were with the sons of men."[37] The handing on of the human form in its verbal image is a central purpose of Pater's art. Like Pico, Pater affirms, through his images, his belief in "a spirit of order and beauty in knowledge, which would come down and unite what men's ignorance had divided, and renew what time had made dim."[38]

CHAPTER FOUR

The House Beautiful
& the Cathedral

Congruous again with the popularity of
the builders of Amiens, of their motives, is
the wealth, the freedom and abundance,
of popular, almost secular, teaching . . .
the Bible treated as a book about men and
women, and other persons equally real,
but blent with lessons, with the liveliest
observations, on the lives of men as they
were then and now, what they do, and
how they do it, or did it then, and on
the doings of nature which so greatly
influence what man does.

Pater, "Notre-Dame d'Amiens"

PATER'S DISCUSSION OF prose in his essay "Style" bears the proprietary impress of one who is talking about his own literary medium. Despite the sometimes defensive tone, the evangelical fervor underlying the exposition communicates Pater's faith in his own contribution to building the House Beautiful. For Pater, prose seems the natural medium to convey modernity, modernity as characterized by complexity and "naturalism"—which are equivalent to relevatism.

> That imaginative prose should be the special and opportune art of the modern world results from two important facts about the latter: first, the chaotic variety and complexity of its interests, making the intellectual issue, the really master currents of the present time incalculable—a condition of mind little susceptible of the restraint proper to verse form, so that the most character- istic verse of the nineteenth century has been law- less verse; and secondly, an all-pervading natural- ism, a curiosity about everything whatever as it really is, involving a certain humility of attitude, cognate to what must, after all, be the less am- bitious form of literature. And prose thus assert- ing itself as the special and privileged artistic faculty of the present day, will be, however critics may try to narrow its scope, as varied in its ex- cellence as humanity itself reflecting on the facts of its latest experience—an instrument of many stops, meditative, observant, descriptive, eloquent, analytic, plaintive, fervid. Its beauties will not be exclusively "pedestrian": it will exert, in due measure, all the varied charms of poetry, down to the rhythm which, as in Cicero, or Michelet, or

Newman, at their best, gives its musical value to
every syllable.[1]

Throughout his work Pater demonstrates an impressive consistency of thought by repetition of ideas or
of metaphors. It may be true that Pater's range of
ideas is quite limited.[2] If so, however, his manipula-
tion of materials into a harmonious whole effectively
makes the points he desires to make. Thus the metaphor
of music in Pater's discussion of prose. As "an instrument of many stops," prose, like the organ, can deliver
the whole orchestration of complexity and can best
interpret a period like the Renaissance, for example.
And the "due measure" of its charms suggests the
imaginative powers of the various forms prose can
take. Likewise, of course, prose serves the humanistic
Pater by being the most effective medium for description of things as they are—in their Romantic grotes-
querie or in their pristine physical charm. Prose, at
least post-Darwinian prose, realizes natural description
better than poetry for the skillful nineteenth-century
practitioner.[3] For Pater, as critic and as creator, the
combination of descriptive powers by which the verbal
artifact can be constructed, and complexity, which the
verbal artifact will manifest, are the paramount virtues
of the prose medium.

Both the critical and the creative functions of the
prose writer work towards realizing the humanist
ideal; for Pater, the ideal means a continuing attempt
to achieve synthesis.[4] The synthesis usually consists of
combining existing artifacts, verbal and otherwise, into
new artifacts—a constant reworking of different com-
binations with the purpose of renewal. "Whatever has
moved man" continues to move him in Pater's esthetic,

but the words may be arranged differently. Criticism and fiction, then, serve the function of revitalizing memory. The relation of the apprehender to the verbal artifact becomes almost a sacramental one, for the associative nature of Pater's work forces the reader to bring his own body of knowledge and experience decisively into play. The movement towards oneness of apprehender and artifact may itself result in synthesis, but the synthesis gives way to a new synthesis as the elements being combined change under the impact of time. Nonetheless, the momentary achievement of synthesis paradoxically defeats time—for a moment. One way of measuring success in life, according to the "Conclusion" to *The Renaissance,* is by enumerating the moments of synthesis,[5] as, for example, Marius does at the moment of his death.

Prose as the vehicle for the human image allows the complexity that makes synthesis possible in the relativistic modern world. Pater presents human images—his verbal artifacts—in situations as characteristically modern as possible to make the reader's response easier. Thus the Renaissance as a period of cultural relativism. *Imaginary Portraits* and the unfinished *Gaston de Latour* likewise have settings in which various streams of thought come together and where an equilibrium of different schemes of values is momentarily achieved.

Of the *Imaginary Portraits,* "Denys L'Auxerrois" demonstrates most clearly Pater's powers of demonstrating a cultural equilibrium in a short tale. "Denys" is, indeed, a fictional realization of the relativism of *The Renaissance,* especially of the balance between pagan and Christian elements. Likewise, *Marius the Epicurean* is Pater's successful effort at realizing his philosophy of culture in longer fiction, *Gaston de Latour* being not-

ably less satisfactory as we now have it. In "Denys
L'Auxerrois" the varieties of cultural experience come
together in Pater's realization of the image of Denys.
Because of the focus on the single character as the
realization of the humanistic ideal, "Denys L'Auxerrois"
has both a compactness and a grotesque quality which
Marius lacks. With less space in which to ratiocinate
about antitheses, Pater forces complexity into a narrow
compass. Synthesis is achieved and then destroyed. Like
"Duke Carl of Rosenmold," the tale serves well as a
fictional realization of Pater's estsetic principles. Just
as the various streams of cultural experience—the
Dionysiac and the Christian—meet only momentarily in
"Denys L'Auxerrois," so the streams of experience in
the reader's mind and in the fiction synthesize only in
the reader's moment of apprehension. The synthesis
then gives way, partly because of time and partly because
of internal pressures.

Pater opens "Denys L'Auxerrois" with a sophisticated
passage alluding to the return of the Greek gods, the
discontent of man, and the futility of regaining Eden
without regaining innocence at the same time:

> Almost every pople, as we know, has had its legend
> of a "golden age" and of its return—legends which
> will hardly be forgotten, however, prosaic the
> world may become, while man himself remains the
> aspiring, never quite contented being he is. And
> yet in truth, since we are no longer children, we
> might well question the advantage of the return
> to us of a condition of life in which, by the nature
> of the case, the values of things would, so to
> speak, lie wholly on their surfaces, unless we could
> regain also the childish consciousness, or rather
> unconsciousness, in ourselves, to take all that
> adroitly and with the appropriate lightness of

heart. The dream, however, has been left for the most part in the usual vagueness of dreams: in their waking hours people have been too busy to furnish it forth with details. What follows is a quaint legend, with detail enough, of such a return of a golden or poetically-gilded age (a denizen of old Greece itself actually finding his way back again among men) as it happened in an ancient town of medieval France.[6]

Denys solves momentarily the problem of discontent, bringing an element of joy into the life of Auxerre. One hears echoes of Blake, whom Pater greatly admired, in the assertion that innocence must be recaptured if man is to apprehend a possible return of the golden age. (In discussing in *The Renaissance* the possibility of recovery, Pater writes that Winckelmann attained the lack of self-consciousness necessarily to appreciate Greek art fully.) Denys, besides being a Dionysus figure, also exhibits for part of his existence a lack of self-consciousness. Pater's story concerns itself with delivering the details of Deny's innocence and of his fall from innocence—the lyric grace and the demonic intensity between which the Dionysiac figures throughout the history of literature and art continually fluctuate.

Auxerre serves well as a setting for the tale of Denys. In it "the products of successive ages, not without lively touches of the present, are blended together harmoniously, with a beauty *specific*. . . ." Pater notes how Turner paints towns like Auxerre in which the river and the town become one in "a perfectly happy conjunction." And the town is "gathered, as if with deliberate aim at such effect, about the central mass of a huge grey catherdral."[7]

The cathedral at Auxerre serves as the center of the

imaginative life of the town and its people; it seems
to symbolize the House Beautiful Pater speaks about
in the "Postscript" to *Appreciations*. The various forces
that center about the cathedral and find representation
in it are cultural or esthetic as well as physical. Pater's
art catholicism—his catholic appreciation of the artistic
manifestations of religion—finds perfect expression in
the cathedral at Auxerre, since the religion practiced
therein encompasses pagan as well as Christian elements,
both exemplified by Denys. The perfect conjunction
of town and river suggests that what goes on in Auxerre
harmonizes with whatever natural order may exist.

Another characteristic of the city fits well into Pater's
relativistic scheme. There is a melancholic strangeness
about the town which recalls Pater's definition of
romanticism:

> Perfect type of that happy mean between northern
> earnestness and the luxury of the south, for which
> we prize midland France, its physiognomy is not
> quite happy—attractive in part for its melancholy.[8]

One can understand readily that Pater's synthesizing
tendencies would make Auxerre a "mean." The melancholia, however, has both Christian and romantic connotations. It is romantic in that it represents an element
of strangeness added to beauty, like the bizarre animals
and the misshapen humans Denys loves.[9] The melancholia is like that found in *The Renaissance* and is a
result of the Christian pointing of the individual's
thoughts towards death. Denys L'Auxerrois himself
assimilates the melancholia only part way through the
story, as he becomes an increasingly Christianized representative of the golden age and acquires self-consciousness.

The tapestries on which Pater's narrator sees the story of Denys, themselves imply a synthesis of the arts. Both the tapestries and the nearby stained glass windows tell the tale of the building of an organ. The organ in the tapestries might be taken for an ideal representation, almost platonic, of the organ standing in the priest's library. Significantly the hearers of the organ in the tapestries dance or shout "as if transported." The result is a "mad vehemence," a sort of "mazy arabesque." In all this, Denys is central; the tapestry exhibits "the various presentations of one oft-repeated figure."[10] The story of Denys as builder of the organ follows, derived from the tapestry and from old records in the priest's "curious library."

The esthetic implications of the tapestry and the tale it tells are many. The prose narrative delivers a description of a tapestry. The tapestry in turn tells the tale of the building of an organ. The prose delivers a pictorial and musical content through the verbal medium, and the realization of one art form in a second which is in turn realized in a third demonstrates clearly how formally interdependent the arts are and how well prose serves as a vehicle for the resultant complexity. The narrative of the tapestry realizes perfectly the esthetics of "The School of Giorgione." The emphasis is on form, and the arts intermingle—becoming, indeed, a complex formal movement. The dance which the narrator describes in the tapestry has its counterpart later in the narrative. Even the events of the story take place in art forms: games, pageants, and divine service. The dance seems the summarizing form: the people of Auxerre in their orgy of fun at the annual ball game and the same people destroying Denys when he takes the role of Winter in the pageant. Pater achieves his aims of realizing a number of esthetic forms through prose and of achieving the movement of his art towards the condition of music.

The recurrence of Denys in all the tapestries results, of course, from Denys being the center of the narrative. The esthetic implication, however, is that Denys represents the human form, the "oft-repeated figure," as it reappears in art under different circumstances and at different times. Like Denys or Dionysus—or the *Mona Lisa* or Duke Carl— it has been dead many times but still recurs in "various presentations." The recurrent human image, in life and in death, dominates. Thus the narrator meets Denys often in the streets in the present, implying a connection between myth, art, and reality —myth begetting art and art begetting reality, which in turn passes back into myth. The myth of Dionysus leads to the tale of Denys. The tale leads the narrator to see Denys in reality.

In "Denys L'Auxerrois," art, myth, and reality cannot be clearly distinguished from one another. Like the generic forms of art—music, painting, prose—they do not isolate themselves nearly so decisively as one might expect. To the twentieth-century reader the boundaries seem indistinct, thanks partly to Pater and his inheritance from his predecessors. But the deliberate blurring of distinctions must have irritated many a polemicist on either side of the controversy about the authenticity of the scriptures. Again one falls back on synthesis as a descriptive term. One thinks of the *Mona Lisa* as a mythical figure, as a work of art, and as a face that appears on the people one meets. Myth, art, and reality exist for Pater only as part of one another. Wilde understood part of Pater's meaning when he asserted that life imitates art. Life also imitates myth (which Pater usually calls legend), myth imitates art, and both myth and art imitate life.

Saint Etienne at Auxerre is a thirteenth-century cathedral. In the manner of the earliest French Renaissance, the sculptors have "a feeling for reality, in no ignoble form, caught, it might seem, from the ardent and full-veined existence then current in these actual streets and houses." The feeling for the human form, like the exemplary quality of the city as a mean between northern and southern European character, identifies Auxerre and its people as representative of Pater's humanism. In the age of cathedrals Pater sees the first stir of the Renaissance. And cultural forces balance in Auxerre. The "narrow, feudal institutions" of the French town change at the time of Denys into "a free, communistic life," of which the cathedral is the symbol. The "figure and character" of Denys stands as "the very genius . . . of that new, free, generous manner in art, active and potent as a living creature."[11]

Pater uses his favorite metaphor of life-in-death and death-in-life to convey the connections between cultures that are to make a rebirth of the golden age possible in Auxerre. The carvers discover a Greek coffin, made for a Roman funeral. The medieval craftsmen sense that the Greek execution is beyond their own capacities, presumably because of the "seriousness of conception" or self-consciousness which attends the medieval workman's carving. The coffin contains "a flask of lively green glass, like a great emerald."[12] Rather than manifesting "ineffable purity," the flask recalls "the riotous and earthly heat of old paganism itself." Certainly the flask recalls the gemlike flame, and the drinking of wine from it becomes the occasion for the return of the golden age. The completion of the mason's work on the cathedral leads to celebration and drinking of the wine. The act of drinking from the pagan flask is very much a sacrament. The flask, the narrator notes, catches the light so dramatically it "might have been 'the wondrous vessel of the Grail.'" The game that follows the sacramental tasting of the wine resembles the dance of the tapestry. Initially the game has "all the decorum of an ecclesiastical ceremony" until Denys appears, for the first time, and makes it more riotous, "really a game."[13]

The implications of Deny's appearance and the effect of the wine are clear. The Dionysiac rite occurs in a Christian setting, and the wine—for all its Christian connotations—brings a loss of self-consciousness that gives the game a freedom it had lacked before. The continuing vitality of the old rite proves itself by the enthusiasm with which the Christian community enters in.

> The boys played like boys, the men almost like madmen, and all with a delightful glee which became contagious, first in the clerical body, and then among the spectators. The aged Dean of the Chapter, Protonotary of his Holiness, held up his purple skirt a little higher, and stepping from the ranks with an amazing levity, as if suddenly relieved of his burden of eighty years, tossed the ball with his foot to the venerable capitulator Homilist, equal to the occasion. And then, unable to stand inactive any longer, the laity carried on the game among themselves, with shouts of ont too boisterous amusement; the sport continuing till the flight

of the ball could no longer be traced along the dusky aisles.[14]

Pater describes the game as a kind of dance in which the participants yield to a force stronger than themselves. Ordered, comely motion with a human focus—Denys—represents the synthesis of two cultures.

"A Study of Dionysus" in *Greek Studies*[15] outlines the importance of physical stimuli, like the wine which arouses Auxerre, in the religion of Dionysus:

> The religion of Dionysus is the religion of people who pass their lives among the vines. As the religion of Demeter carries us back to the cornfields and farmsteads of Greece, and places us, in fancy, among a primitive race, in the furrow and beside the granary; so the religion of Dionysus carries us back to its vineyards, and is a monument of the ways and thoughts of people whose days go by beside the winepress, and under the green and purple shadows, and whose material happiness depends on the crop of grapes. For them the thought of Dionysus and his circle, a little Olympus outside the greater, covered the whole of life, and was a complete religion, a sacred representation or interpretation of the whole human experience, modified by the special limitations, the special privileges of insight or suggestion, incident to their peculiar mode of existence.[16]

The countryside of Auxerre resembles the land of the vine in Greece, but more important the religion springs from physical causes. Just as Pater's Marius associates his deities with particular places around his home and just as he later comes to apprehend the Christian god in the phenomena of the liturgy, so the worshippers

of Dionysus draw their insight from their countryside
and from the physical world in which they pass their
days. Their god takes on the characteristics of the
ground which gave him birth, a point Pater makes
particularly clear in "Denys L'Auxerrois."

The Dionysiac religion can reappear in Auxerre not
merely because the natural conditions are the same,
but because the old religion, like all things which have
once moved the human mind, has become a dormant
artifact waiting to be exhumed and revivified, as it
is in the person of Denys. The Greek flask represents
the dead religion waiting to spring back to life, the
wine it contains being as potent as when it filled the
Greek sculptors who made the coffin in which it rests.
In his analysis of the religion of Dionysus in Greece,
Pater comments on both the continuing vitality of the
Dionysiac idea and its associative representation in the
human form of the god:

> Now, if the reader wishes to understand what the
> scope of the religion of Dionysus was to the Greeks
> who lived in it, all it represented to them by way
> of one clearly conceived yet complex symbol, let
> him reflect what the loss would be if all the effect
> and expression draw from the imagery of the vine
> and the cup fell out of the whole body of existing
> poetry; how many fascinating trains of reflexion,
> what colour and substance would therewith have
> been deducted from it, filled as it is, apart from the
> more aweful associations of the Christian ritual,
> apart from Galahad's cup, with all the various
> symbolism of the fruit of the vine. That supposed
> loss is but an imperfect measure of all that the
> name of Dionysus recalled to the Greek mind,
> under a single imaginable form, an outward body

of flesh presented to the senses, and comprehending, as its animating soul, a whole world of
thoughts, surmises, greater and less experiences.[17]

"Denys L'Auxerrois" might be said to be the fictional
realization of Pater's critique, bringing out all the
humanistic and anthropomorphic implications in the
setting of Auxerre.

The myth of Dionysus was useful to Pater for another reason. His humanism focuses very much on the
idea of death, on pain. The Dionysiac death, with its
fearful rending of the body and its subsequent rebirth,
fits well into Pater's humanist philosophy; the human
form in art suffers and dies again and again, but it is
reborn as often as it dies, to begin the cycle again.
Pater could accept death as a kind of refining process
through which the human or the image of the human
must go in order to attain a new and fuller being.

In *Appreciations,* Pater makes this point when writing of Sir Thomas Browne:

> He is writing [in *Urn-Burial*] in a very complex
> situation—to a friend, upon occasion of the death
> of a common friend. The deceased apparently had
> been little known to Browne himself till his recent
> visits, while the intimate friend to whom he is
> writing had been absent at the time; and the lead-
> ing motive of Browne's letter is the deep impression
> he has received during those visits, of a sort of
> physical beauty in the coming of death, with which
> he still surprises and moves his reader. There had
> been, in this case, a tardiness and reluctancy in the
> circumstances of dissolution, which had permitted
> him, in the character of a physician, as it were to
> assist at the spiritualising of the bodily frame by

natural process; a wonderful new type of mortified
grace being evolved by the way. The spiritual body
had anticipated the formal moment of death; the
alert soul, in that tardy decay, changing its vesture
gradually, as if piece by piece. The infinite future
had invaded this life perceptibly to the sense, like
the ocean felt far inland up a tidal river. Nowhere,
perhaps, is the attitude of questioning awe on the
threshold of another life displayed with the ex-
pressiveness of this unique morsel of literature . . .
so strangely! the visible function of death is but to
refine, to detach from aught that is vulgar.[18]

Using Sir Thomas Browne as his text, Pater reverses
the life-death cycle for his own purposes: the purer
existence, even in the physical sense, follows death.
The wine in the Greek coffin at Auxerre has much
sediment and increased potency, and the picture of
Denys is, at least for the purposes of the story, more
lively and more beautiful than the god Dionysus. Pater
does not push his argument to the point of asserting
that the refined condition of the body comes from its
treatment by Browne in prose, but he does refer to the
complexity of the situation, meaning, of course, that
there were contraries to be resolved. And Browne does
become the conveyor through prose of the beauty of
the dying form, even as he participates in the process
of death as physician. Sir Thomas Browne might be
said to be the priest who administers an exteme unction
that releases the body rather than the soul and assimilates it into the realm of art.

Denys is not the only one of Pater's figures who seems
to spring from a coffin. (Denys appears immediately
after the coffin with the flask is discovered, and although he has an antecedent history, the implication

is that his realization as a Dionysiac figure depends upon
the finding of the coffin with its wine; without it, there
would have been no story of Denys.) Emerald Uthwart
leaves his coffin in France to return to England. One
of Pater's favorite incidents in the novels of the Brontës
is Heathcliffe's effort to lie in Catherine Linton's grave:

> Much later, in a Yorkshire village, the spirit of
> romanticism bore a more really characteristic fruit
> in the work of a young girl, Emily Brontë, the
> romance of *Wuthering Heights;* the figures of
> Hareton Earnshaw, of Catherine Linton, and of
> Heathcliffe—tearing open Catherine's grave, remov-
> ing one side of her coffin, that he may really lie
> beside her in death—figures so passionate, yet
> woven on a background of delicately beautiful,
> moorland scenery, being typical examples of that
> spirit.[19]

Reversal of argument is one of Pater's frequent tech-
niques, and the example from *Wuthering Heights* shows
a living man yearning for death-in-life as a means of
unifying himself with his mistress, who, presumably,
has attained a kind of life-in-death. The passage on
Wuthering Heights also suggests that Pater understands
his own preoccupation with the human form as corpse
to be part of his romantic inheritance. And in his use
of the tapestry metaphor (the scene in Yorkshire is
described as woven) Pater gives another example of the
sort of synthesizing of the arts he accomplishes in "Denys
L'Auxerrois."[20]

When Denys enters into the life of Auxerre, he brings
a salutary influence that parallels the effect of art on
life. Always focusing on the human form, Pater's
narrator notes that it was a period "of young men and

their influence."²¹ The new communal life resembles the Renaissance in its cultural freedom, its exchange of ideas. And under the impress of Denys the humanistic element becomes dominant in Auxerre, much as it does in modern life under the influence of art.

> One man engaged with another in talk in the market-place; a new influence came forth at the contact; another and then another adhered; at last a new spirit was abroad everywhere.²²

The new spirit emphasizes the Dionysiac side of humanism, but it has a moral purpose: "the cultivation, for their due service to man, of delightful natural things." There is a constant movement back and forth between physical and metaphysical, between artistic and natural: Denys seems born out of the coffin that contained the wine flask; his influence leads to a new cultivation of "natural things"; games become really games rather than rituals symbolizing something else; and the hunting of Denys through the streets at the story's conclusion ends in a real death rather than a mock one.

Pater, for all his Hellenic sympathies, also values the virtues of the medieval Christian civilization. In "Denys L'Auxerrois," Pater shows how unhealthy the dominance of one idea can be to any civilization. The Dionysiac revels that possess the town and which finally drive Denys half mad symbolize the exclusive dominance of one idea: the golden age lasts only briefly, only so long as equilibrium is maintained. When Christian values begin to be forgotten, the clergy of Auxerre, Denys's patrons, seek a solution. What they settle on is what might be expected of Pater. They do not attempt to promulgate a new Christian doctrine or issue solemn calls to worship. They exhume the body of a saint. The Christian idea is subsumed in the human image, which, in Pater's philosophy of culture, is the principal vehicle of metaphysical thought.

The exhumation symbolizes, then, the reintroduction of Christianity into the society of Auxerre, and from the moment of the exhumation Denys's fate is sealed. Paganism gives way to renewed Christianity which for a time influences Denys. Denys's book illustrations become more serious, "as if the gay old pagan world had been *blessed* in some way."[23] An organ is built; only the Apollo painted on the shutters disapproves of it, perhaps because of the opposition between the Appollonian and Dionysiac spirits, but also possibly because of the Christianizing of the pagan musical instrument.[24] (Denys's instrument is the characteristic reed, as Apollo's is the lyre. The organ, being a wind instrument, would not be favored by Apollo.) Denys decides to exhume the body of his own mother and to rebury it near the cloister as an effort both to consecrate her remains and to renew his own waning life. The incident, of course, has its parallel in the Dionysus myth, but Pater's reworking of the myth to place emphasis on the body itself is significant. (Dionysus in the myth brings his mother back from the underworld.) Only his mother's bones remain, and renewal does not come, at least not in the form that might have been expected.

After the reinterment of the bones of Denys's mother, there follows the first trial of the organ. Denys, the builder, plays the organ, and later in the evening meets his death playing the part of Winter in a pageant of the "hunting of the unholy creature."[25] On the oc-

casion of the trial of the organ and the games, a new
lord comes to reign over Auxerre. He is a "goodly
young man"; he comes to wed Lady Ariane (Dionysus's Ariadne) who had formerly favored Denys. He
represents the new human image around which the
life of Auxerre will center as it once centered around
Denys—he is the focus of its existence and indeed is
but another manifestation of the natural form that
gives life to art and society. When Denys dies, he must
replace Denys as one of those "images that yet fresh
images beget." Thus Pater's narrator sees Denys on
the streets, sometimes tortured—fittingly enough, since
he represents both the pain and the pleasure in human
existence. Just as Hyacinth in "Apollo in Picardy"
receives a new existence through the flowers that bear
his name, so Denys lives on in the human forms that
come and go in Auxerre. He continues to dominate,
however his image is clad.[26] His pagan instrument continues to play Christian music in the all-embracing
cathedral.

It is easy to see why for Pater the acceptance of the
full flow of experience, the complete world of art,
becomes an almost religious experience. In "Denys
L'Auxerrois" Pater brings paganism into the Christian
church precisely to show that fullness of life—which
the cathedral, in its central position in the life of the
community, should represent—cannot be exclusive. It
cannot be exclusive even of the pagan mode of thought
that seems to be its contrary. When the cathedral fulfills
its function as inclusive center of communal life and
art, it becomes the physical symbol of the House
Beautiful.

One recalls that in *The Renaissance,* Winckelmann

comes to the Vatican as a nominal Christian specifically to appreciate the pagan artifacts the Vatican has to offer.[27] Winckelmann's approach to the things he finds is openly sensual, just as Marius's response to the early Christian religious rites is sensual. The intermingling of pagan and Christian sentiment in the House Beautiful signifies not only the extension into the world of art of Pater's relevatism but also an extension into religion of the sensual.

In *Gaston de Latour,* for example, Pater emphasizes necessary connections between the living people who inhabit the ecclesiastical buildings at Chartres and the inanimate and natural objects around them. The boys with whom Gaston studies and plays are a case in point:

> Here and now, at all events, carrying their cheer-ful tumult through all those quiet ecclesiastical places—the bishop's garden, the great sacristy, neat and clean in its brown, pensive lights, they seemed of a piece with the bright, simple, inanimate things, the toys, of nature. They made one lively picture with the fruit and wine they loved, the birds they captured, the buckets of clear water drawn for pastime from the great well, and Jean Sémur's painted conjuring book stolen from the old sorceress, his grandmother, out of which he told their fortunes; with the musical instruments of others; with their carefully hidden dice and playing-cards, worn or soiled by the fingers of the older gamesters who had discarded them. Like their elders, they read eagerly, in racy, new trans-lations, old Greek and Latin books, with a delight-ful shudder at the wanton paganism. It was a new element of confusion in the presentiment of that miniature world. . . . Above all, in natural,

heartfelt kinship with their own violent though
refined and cunning time, they loved every incident
of soldiering; while the changes of the year, the
lights, the shadows, the flickering fires of winter,
with which Gaston had first associated his companions, so full of artificial enjoyment for the well-
to-do, added themselves pleasantly, by way of shifting background, to the spectacular effort.[28]

The discussion of the boys at Chartres (which precedes the discussion of Gaston's reaction to the physical
world) is one of many examples of Pater's synthesizing
mind and repetitive style. The oneness of man with
nature and with made objects remind us of "An English
Poet" and of Marius's experience with nature at White-
nights, of Denys l'Auxerrois's appearance in tapestry
and of his appearance in life to the narrator of his tale.
Jean Sémur's "painted conjuring book" resembles the
ancient and occult documents into which Pico della
Mirandola delves. Music, typically, enters into their
life, and there is a discreet concealment of such pec-
cadilloes as playing cards.[29] Harmony—principally a
visual harmony—predominates.

The soldiering, which appears in "Emerald Uthwart"
and in various of the *Imaginary Portraits,* reflects Pater's
concern for the visual impression. The changeability
of the visual impression, so important a characteristic
of the various responses which man has to the scene
before him, seems to dominate the mind of Gaston as
he thinks about his fellows. Most significant, however,
is the reference to the life at Chartres as representing
a "miniature world." Thus the cathedral is representative of the great world outside itself, the place where
art, nature, and human life become one, where appre-

hended and apprehender are indistingishable. As always, "in the *House Beautiful*" there are no exclusions.[30]

In the cathedral of Chartres—a late medieval version of the House Beautiful—the humanistic impulse is very much alive. Not only the living but also the dead are about in plentiful supply:

> That lavish display of jewellers' work on the altars, in the chapels, the sacristies, of Our Lady's Church was but a framing for little else than dead people's bones. . . . The abundant relics of the church of Chartres were for the most part perished remnants of the poor human body itself; but appertaining to persons long ago and of a far-off, immeasureable kind of sanctity, stimulated a more indifferent sort of curiosity, and seemed to bring the distant, the impossible, as with tangible evidence of fact, close to one's side. It was in one's hand—the finger of an Evangelist![31]

The cathedral as House Beautiful has not only a contemporary inclusiveness, taking something from every part of the varied life of the community about it, but also a historical inclusiveness, connecting itself with the epochs that have gone before. And the point of connection as in "Denys L'Auxerrois," is the human form.

The closeness between fiction and criticism in Pater is illustrated by the comparative evaluations of the cathedrals of Chartres and Amiens. The cathedral evoked in Pater's critical essay "Notre-Dame d'Amiens" closely resembles the Chartres given us in *Gaston de Latour*. The cathedral at Amiens is the "greatest and purest of Gothic churches." And, like Chartres, it is the site of a humanistic flowering in the late Middle Ages.

> The Charter of Amiens served as the model for many other communes. Notre-Dame d'Amiens is the church of a commune. In that century of Saint Francis, of Saint Louis, they were still religious. But over against monastic interests, as identified with a central authority—king, emperor, or pope—they pushed forward the local, and, so to call it, secular authority of their bishops, the flower of the "secular clergy" in all its mundane astuteness, ready enough to make their way as the natural protectors of such townships. The people of Amiens, for instance, under a powerful episcopal patron, invested their civic pride in a vast cathedral, outrivalling neighbours, as being in effect their parochial church, and promoted there the new, revolutionary, Gothic manner, at the expense of the derivative and traditional, Roman or Romanesque, style, the imperial style, of the great monastic churches. Nay, those grand and beautiful *people's* churches of the thirteenth century, churches pre-eminently of "Our Lady," concurred also with certain novel humanistic movements of religion itself at that period, above all with the expansion of what is reassuring and popular in the worship of Mary, as a tender and accessible, though almost irresistible, intercessor with her severe and awful son.[32]

Amiens appeals to Pater as much for its extra-religious as for its religious characteristics. Far from being "monastic," it is communal and the bishop is a member of the "secular clergy." Christ appears in the passage as severe judge and Mary as gracious intercessor, the adoration of the latter being characteristic

of the broadening sympathies of the no-longer-exclusive
spirit of the later Middle Ages and a congenial subject
for Pater's analysis.

Characteristically, Pater emphasizes the humanism
in the ornamentation of Amiens:

> Congruous again with the popularity of the
> builders of Amiens, of their motives, is the wealth,
> the freedom and abundance, of popular, almost
> secular, teaching, here afforded, in the carving
> especially, within and without; and open Bible,
> in place of later legend, as at monastic Vézelay,—
> the Bible treated as a book about men and women,
> and other persons equally real, but blent with
> lessons, with the liveliest observations, on the lives
> of men as they were then and now, what they do,
> and how they do it, or did it then, and on the
> doings of nature which so greatly influence what
> man does; . . . Above all, it is to be observed that
> as a result of this free spirit, in it, art has at last
> become personal. The artist, as such, appears at
> Amiens, as elsewhere, in the thirteenth century.
> . . . He is no longer a Byzantine, but a Greek—an
> unconscious Greek.[33]

It is typical that Pater should stress the connections
between the art of a cathedral he admires and "real"
men and women. His assertion that the artists of
Amiens are Greek in spirit fits nicely into his historical
framework: the waning Middle Ages and the coming
Renaissance are characterized by an increasingly pagan
or humanistic spirit, and the artist who senses the
changes in the cultural life around him responds by
asserting his own identity. His work becomes more
freely referential to life and his treatment of conven-
tions becomes more imaginative. Unlike Yeats, Pater

shows little interest in the Byzantine, and the movement of painting and sculpture away from the Byzantine style in the twelfth, thirteenth, and fourteenth centuries must have seemed to Pater a distinctly beneficial result of the rebirth of interest in the classical world. One may surmise that the static quality of Byzantine art could not have appealed much to a critic whose esthetic includes as a premise the constancy of change in the artist's approach to his subject matter. For Pater, the Byzantine artist could hardly have been a humanist, for he seemed to have neither sufficient identity as an individual nor sufficient ability to modify his art to fit his changing conception of the world about him.

The static and nonhumanistic approach to art manifests itself in Vézelay, a Romanesque monastic church to which Pater responds with reserve and a little sorrow. The art of Vézelay, like that of other churches of the Cistercian order, does not link itself to humanity. "Bold, crude, original, their [the sculptors of Vézelay's] work indicates delight in the power of reproducing fact, curiosity in it, but little or no sense of beauty." Even the beauty of the columns derives from a kind of imaginative fantasy rather than from reference to the beauty of the world about:

> Man and morality, however, disappearing at intervals, the acanthine capitals have a kind of later Venetian beauty about them, as the Venetian birds also, the conventional peacocks, or birds wholly of fantasy, amid the long fantastic foliage. There are still however, no true flowers of the field here.[34]

Pater goes on to note that any sculpture other than the rather grotesque carvings at Vézelay would have been practically invisible in the darkened, "sombre" interior. The pall of the interior becomes the prevailing impression Pater has of the church.

In spite of the virtues of the building—its state of preservation is almost as fresh as that of some Greek temples—Vézelay conveys the feeling of exclusiveness and doctrinaire authority:

> And yet . . . the *Madeleine* of Vézelay is still preeminently a Romanesque, and thereby the typically monastic, church. In spite of restoration even, as we linger here, the imuression of the monastic Middle Age, of a very exclusive monasticism, that has verily turned its back upon common life, jealously closed inward upon itself, is a singularly weighty one; the more so because, as the peasant said when asked the way to an old sanctuary that had fallen to the occupation of farm-labourers, and was now deserted even by them: *Maintenant il n'y a personne là.*[35]

Pater makes his point quite explicitly by use of the French equivalent for *no one:* literally and etymologically there is no *person* at Vézelay. It is the cathedral emptied of its humanistic content, therefore, not a House Beautiful.

Pater's House Beautiful and the cathedrals he chooses as parallels for his esthetic structure—for example, Auxerre—are humanistic in their relevance to man. They accept the various components of life about them, the various human manifestations—and in doing so they are also relativistic. For relativism, like any other "metaphysical" idea, takes on meaning for Pater when it is associated with man. Pater's relativism, indeed, becomes at times part of the fabric of his humanism,

The cathedral demonstrates this fact about Pater's thought more than any explicitly stated argument. The worldly symbol of the House Beautiful, the cathedral serves its highest purpose—as at Amiens and Chartres—only in its continuing openness to the human life about it.

CHAPTER FIVE

The Hard, Gemlike Flame in Aurelian Rome

To him the sustained stillness without seemed really but to be waiting upon that interior, mental condition of preparation or expectancy, for which he was just then intently striving.

Pater, *Marius the Epicurean*

LIKE 'THE RENAISSANCE,' *Marius the Epicurean* may be described as circular. *The Renaissance* begins in medieval France with a Christianity of pagan inclinations and ends in Rome with a German critic who has made his pilgrimage to the capital of Christendom to see the pagan artifacts there. *Marius* begins with a pagan childhood full of Christian overtones and ends with an almost-Christian death of which the principal celebrated virtues are pagan.

The two books have other similarities. Both depend on an intensity of visual imagination for their most effective realizations of their subjects. For all his bows to the tactile values of sculpture and for all his use of the metaphor of music, truth remains for Pater consistently a visual quality. Equally important, Pater's evocation of Aurelian Rome shows it to be as much a synthesis of varying modes of thought and expression as the Renaissance itself.

But Pater uses a more intricate structure in *Marius* than in *The Renaiassnce*. The synthesis is given a presiding genius, Marcus Aurelius, whose most striking and paradoxical characteristic is his lack of interest in the spectacles going on around him. (Even Marcus Aurelius, however, must be drawn into Pater's favorite kind of dramatic incident, the confrontation with death as it strikes a beloved person, in this case Aurelius's son.) And the adventurous spirit, Marius, is given a guide. As critic Pater is very much present in *The Renaissance;* in *Marius* the omnipresence of the author as a philosopher of culture is less obvious. Marius (the personification of the reader of *The Renaissance,* among other things) has a companion who directs his thoughts.

The companion constantly shifts his physical form and his philosophical allegiance with the passing of time; the young physician at the temple of Aesculapius, Flavian, Cornelius, and even the young soldier who befriends Marius in the last chapter may be considered different embodiments of the "divine companion" Pater speaks about.

> Companionship, indeed, familiarity with others, gifted in this way or that, or at least pleasant to him, had been, through one or another long span of it, the chief delight of the journey. And was it only the resultant general sense of such familiarity, diffused through his memory, that in a while suggested the question whether there had not been—besides Flavian, besides Cornelius even, and amid the solitude which in spite of ardent friendship he had loved best of all things—some other unfailing companion, ever at his side throughout; doubling his pleasure in the roses by the way, patient of his peevishness or depression, sympathetic above all with his grateful recognition, onward from his earliest days, of the fact that he was there at all?[1]

Further on we learn more about the "divine companion":

> That divine companion figured no longer as but an occasional wayfarer beside him; but rather as the unfailing "assistant," without whose inspiration and concurrence he could not breathe or see, instrumenting his bodily senses, rounding, supporting his imperfect thoughts.[2]

There is certainly the suggestion that the companion partakes of each "real" companion Marius has known, partly through the powers of Marius's memory which are to be so vividly sharpened at the end of the book. Granting the theological importance of the "divine companion"—and Pater's desire to give some theological backing to his purpose of public *apologia*—the concept has a central esthetic function.[3] It unites the various strains in Marius's experience and gives moral sanction to his choices, accomplishing both of these things while seeming to be Christian. Marius's ever-so-slightly shifting philosophical allegiances are closely tied to the tutelary spirit of the moment. For Pater a tutelary spirit can exist only in bodily form. Marius beholds and believes, always tying himself to the visual impression. One of the features of Marius's consistency throughout the book is that he depends very much on his eyes for the nourishment of his mind. His Cyrenaicism acknowledges varying philosophical possibilities, but each possibility must be one that Marius can behold.

To some extent, of course, Pater's fictional method represents an evasion of commitments which his contemporaries were apt to find annoying or frustrating. J. A. Symonds approached the reading of *Marius* with the trepidation that might be expected of a belligerent cultural historian who had had the public largely to himself for ten years. Pater's sometime competitor laments, in a letter to Henry Sidgwick, the necessity of undertaking the novel:

> 'Marius' I have not read. I suppose I must. But I shrink from approaching Pater's style, which has a peculiarly disagreeable effect upon my nerves —like the presence of a civet cat. Still, I believe I must read it.[4]

Symonds's privately-disclosed reaction remains that of most post-Victorian readers, for whom reading *Marius* was at best a dubious duty and certainly not a pleasure. Admittedly Pater's style often seems obfuscatory, more obscurantist than evocative. The "Well!" which comes along with distressing frequency to promise more than it delivers can hardly be considered anything but an annoying piece of stylistic self-indulgence. Yet the book hardly deserves this response. Pater certainly intended *Marius* to be an inviting vehicle for his philosophical and esthetic missionary work as well as an expedient *apologia* (too eagerly accepted by his contemporaries at what seemed to be face value) for his life and opinions.

A principle evident throughout Pater's writings which readers must accept is that of statement through suggestion or reiteration or visual description. Pater could not offer Symonds a clearly worded historical novel with easily perceived allegiances, like Shorthouse's *John Inglesant,* nor as well-researched reconstruction of an earlier culture, like some of Symonds's own volumes. Pater works at his best when his ground seems to be shifting almost from moment to moment; the reader must accept the extensive qualifications of one statement or another as both acceptable and necessary in a writer whose purpose is to avoid decisive commitments.

One frequently finds the suggestion that Pater's main motive in writing *Marius* was to trace his personal philosophical development.[5] Having supposedly progressed beyond the epicureanism of the "Conclusion" to *The Renaissance,* Pater, according to some critics, sets out to give a depiction of his philosophy of life as it stood in the early 1880s. So runs the argument. Pater completed the book in 1883 or 1884,[6] and it was taken by his admirers as an affirmation of his acceptance of Christianity. Some critics see *Marius* as a movement by Pater towards Christianity; others see the book as an indication of Pater's movement away from the philosophy of the "Conclusion."[7]

The biographical emphasis has done Pater a disservice. The implication of the critical consensus is that *Marius* is chiefly of interest as a document illustrating Pater's philosophical development. The biographical approach may be accounted for in two ways. First, the supposed perversion by his disciples of Pater's dicta in the "Conclusion" has led well-meaning apologists to seek other dicta in *Marius*. Second, the dearth of events in Pater's life—aside from the assortment of curious and often meaningless anecdotes offered by Wright—leads those critics interested in biography to trace Pater's philosophical development. Both reasons find some encouragement, conscious in one case, from Pater himself.[8] One cannot doubt that Pater intended *Marius* to correct the impression the public at large had of his estheticism and to make his philosophy of culture more respectable.

The appropriateness of a biographical approach to *Marius* cannot be denied, but the emphasis in such an analysis would be better placed on continuity rather than on change of philosophical position.[9] Pater's desire to correct the public impression has been taken too readily as representative of a substantial change in his position. *Marius,* in both the first edition and the later revision, modifies Pater's stance less than it seems to and in fact is the logical working out of the philosophy of the "Conclusion."

In demonstrating the reasons for Pater's suppression of the "Conclusion," Geoffrey Tillotson gives by implication a good reason for the writing of *Marius.* Tillotson asserts that the suppression of the "Conclusion" stems from Pater's reaction to the public estimate of his philosophy.[10] Mallock's *The New Republic* had appeared in 1877. Pater appears in the novel as the sensual, almost obscene Mr. Rose, but the often-cited example of Mr. Rose's talking of people "as if they had no clothes on" is not half so damaging as Mr. Rose's ecstatic references to such famous pairs as Damon and Pythias and David and Jonathan.[11] The satire disturbed Pater. Combined with the flamboyance of Pater's self-declared and only half-accepted disciple Wilde, Mallock's portrait influenced Pater to suppress the "Conclusion" in the second edition of *The Renaissance.*[12] The decision to write *Marius* has similar origins. Pater wrote the book not so much to indicate a change in his philosophy—no such change can be demonstrated from the text—as to cast that philosophy in a mode more acceptable to his contemporaries. Reputation was important to the reticent don,[13] and *Marius* serves the double purpose of redefining Pater's philosophic position in terms less easily subject to oversimplification and of providing an opportunity for the realization of the philosophic position in imaginative form.

Pater himself provides a good critical guide to an appreciation of *Marius* in his evaluation of Plato's *Republic* in *Plato and Platonism*. For Pater, Plato makes art of philosophy and the *Republic* becomes a philosophical *jeu d'esprit*. The range of ideas in the dialogues and particularly in the *Republic* is so great that realization of all of them requires a withdrawal from specific commitment on the part of the author:

> The absolute and eternal character, of such ideas involved, with much labour and scruple, repeated

138

acts of qualification and correction; many read-
justments to experience; expansion by larger lights
from it; those exclusions and inclusions, *debitae
naturae* (to repeat Bacon's phrase) demanded, that
is to say, by the veritable nature of the facts which
those ideas are designed to represent.[14]

The emphasis falls on qualification, correction, and
readjustment, rather than on "the absolute and eternal
character" of the ideas. Thus the Platonic dialogue as
a literary form and the *Republic* itself. Pater quotes
from Plato:

Suffer me, he says, to entertain myself as men of
listless minds are wont to do when they journey
alone. Such persons, I fancy, before they have
found out in what way ought of what they desire
may come to be, pass that question by lest they
grow weary in considering whether the thing be
possible or no; and supposing what they wish already achieved, they proceed at once to arrange all
the rest, pleasing themselves in the tracing out all
they will do, when that shall have come to pass—
making a mind already idle idler still.[15]

One of the things characteristic of Pater that one finds
in the quotation is the emphasis on the need for time
and reflection—as opposed to "idleness"—to develop a
complex mode of thought.

Pater sees in Plato a series of alternatives offered to
the searcher for the absolute. The search (the "means"
of Pater's essay on Wordsworth) supersedes the absolute itself (the "end") in Pater's reading. The quotation
from Plato indicates dissatisfaction with the view that
all experience must be understood from a static philosophical position. The "idle mind" arranges experience

in narrow categories deriving from one strict philosophy and thus ignores the responsibility to test the philosophy and to try alternatives. The passage can be understood by reference to Pater's repeated invocation of light in his essays. Light, as it illuminates a made object or a natural scene, constantly changes. The gemlike flame also is illusive, many-faceted; it is always bright but it is always changing. The idle mind, like a cold, unchanging light, centers on only one object; it never achieves the desirable goal of variety or alternation.

It is not only the interwoven passages from classical literature that connect *Marius* with the world of Plato.[16] *Marius* itself is a kind of dialogue; a number of philosophical positions are expounded, juxtaposed, and compared. The effect seems more variation, alternation, than development. Like the *Republic,* as Pater sees it, *Marius* offers something for persons of any persuasion; it is chameleonlike; its reputation, indeed, is a lesson in alternative interpretations.

Pater opens the novel with a calculated bow to Christianity that serves an esthetic purpose, as well as the public purpose of making *Marius* acceptable to a late-Victorian, partly Christian public. Just as late paganism lingered longest in the country during the advent of Christianity, the "old religion," the purer form of paganism, lingered on in the country during the breakup of the Greco-Roman religion into a complex series of cults. Pater gives the "earlier and simpler patriarchial religion, 'the religion of Numa,' " an edenic setting.[17] Seemingly isolated from the flow of events around it, the old religion of Marius's childhood is subject to "little change" in its pastoral surroundings. The Christianity of England in the nineteenth century, the religion Pater knew most intimately as a child and as a young man, endured similarly in the country, or so Pater thinks, as Darwinianism and relativism began to command the allegiance of the most sophisticated minds. The flux operates at later times and in other places for Marius. His childhood has the advantage of repose.

The "sacred equity" of Marius's childhood religion time and again begins to resemble a form of Christianity. The use of bread and wine and oil combine with a dozen nuances of expression to suggest the Christian rather than the pagan to the nineteenth-century reader. Pater's purpose at every point—and the early chapters of *Marius* are no exception—can be understood better if one remembers that his view of religion in *The Renaissance* is an anti-dogmatic one. As elsewhere, Pater tries at the beginning of *Marius* to convey the physical phenomena upon which religion depends and to suggest thereby the close connections between a Christianity and a paganism which have little in common doctrinally. For the more ingenuous of his readers, Pater is merely providing an anticipation of later Christianity in early paganism. For the more subtle, he is asserting that the best elements of each are liturgical or more broadly ceremonial rather than doctrinal, and that paganism can be as 'pure' and appealing as Christianity. The latter effect he accomplishes by making the life at White-nights highly moral, intensely sympathetic. If the reader accepts the idyllic life there, he must also accept the paganism upon which the idyllic life is based.

At one point Pater suggests that "glimpses" of the survival of the old religion may be perceived beneath the artifices of Latin pastoral poetry. Tibullus, using "repetitions of a consecrated form of words," seems to capture the essence of the old liturgy in his elegies.[18] Certainly, our attention is directed momentarily to Pater's own medium, prose, to his elegiac tone (Pater is always mourning the passing of his happiest moments, even when they are at their point of fullest realization), to his favorite rhetorical device, the repetition of words meaningful because of their appearance throughout his works. Pater is particularly sensitive to liturgical style, where words take on their meaning from their repeated use in shifting contexts. One immediately senses Pater's preference for a "religion of usages and sentiments rather than of facts and beliefs."[19] The "quiet people" who prefer such a religion find the reticent Pater's favor. Suitable analogies between Pater's own life and the life of the folk adhering to the "religion of Numa" can be found easily enough, not only in his reticence and dislike of dogma but also in his regular attendance at chapel and in his fondness for the religious forms practiced at St. Austin's priory.[20] Like Pater, the protagonist of the novel is one of the "quiet people."

Marius reminds us of other typical Pater heroes in having "a spontaneous force of religious veneration . . . a native instinct of devotion."[21] In this religious instinct, he resembles the unnamed English poet, Duke Carl of Rosenmold, and Winckelmann. Mrs. Humphrey Ward, who gives us the firm connection between the suppression of the "Conclusion" and the writing of *Marius,* also points out the relevance of "The Child in the House" to the latter.[22] Mrs. Ward considers Marius the completion of a project of which "The Child in the House" was the unsatisfactory beginning. The connections between the early chapters of *Marius* and the biographical fantasy are quite evident. Like *Marius,*

Florian Deleal spends his early days in a demi-paradise; "the sense of security could hardly have been deeper."[23] Although close to a town, Florian's house has a rural setting "among high garden-wall, bright all summer-time with the Golden-rod and brown-and-golden Wall-flower."[24] Like Marius, Florian Deleal apprehends the world around him with a "complex spiritual habit." And like the adherents of the "religion of Numa," whose worship is "attached to very definite places and things," Florian Deleal assigns more importance to the "sensible vehicle or occasion" of abstract thought than to abstract thought itself.

The parallel between the two works is as important for the light it throws on *Marius* as for the philosophical consistency it demonstrates. The later lives of both Marius and Florian Deleal bear the imprint of the early home life, and the early impressions of home finally determine Marius's course as he decides to sacrifice himself. The edenic setting gives both Marius and Florian Deleal a "sustained stillness," the "mental condition of preparation or expectancy," which readies them for striking impressions to be apprehended later in life. But it also gives them the taste for repose, the security of the closed circle, and having once experienced the demi-paradise, neither can fully divorce himself from a desire to return. The idealized childhood religion forms the base for the philosophical structure of the novel.

The spiritual adventures of Marius center about three principal confrontations: with Cyrenaicism, with Stoicism, and with Christianity. Marius accepts Cyrenaicism, represented by Flavian, after abandoning the old religion, which dies with his mother; he considers and rejects Stoicism; and he accepts parts of Christianity, represented by Cornelius. These points of reference within the movement of the novel do not, of course, tell the whole tale of Marius, for the shadings of his commitments and rejections are legion. Usually the commitments and rejections are based on the psychological impact of what Marius sees. The scene in the arena repels Marius because he *sees* it (and sees Marcus Aurelius ignoring it), not because of any philosophical repugnance to what is going on. His eye, not his mind, is sympathetic.

Just as the first two chapters, concerning Marius's home life, provide the background necessary to the understanding of what happens afterwards, the third chapter, "Change of Air," shows the reader Marius's first confrontation of life outside his family circle and his response to it. The chapter has not attracted the interest of critics very much, but its importance cannot be overestimated, for in it Marius becomes conscious of his dependence on visual reality and of his capacity for intense emotional attachment.

In "Change of Air" Marius is taken for the cure of "some boyish sickness" to a temple of Aesculapius among the Etrurian hills. Pater suggests early in the chapter that the religion of bodily health is the most important surviving part of the old paganism and furthermore that the cult of Aesculapius is very much like the Christian priesthood. Through dreams inspired by Aesculapius, the sufferer may be directed to his cure, and Marius, under the care of the priests, is thus cured. At one point Marius, having slept feverishly, awakes to find a youth beside him and to find his fever passing. The appearance of the youth, who enters the room with a torch, impresses itself upon Marius's mind and from this moment on he acknowledges the ascendancy of visual reality. In the very appearance of the young man there is some healing power, perhaps analogous to the effect of the human form in art on the beholder. Marius recovers. During the remainder of his stay, he takes walks about the grounds, learning more about Aesculapius and about the symbol of the snake with which, to Marius's discomfort, Aesculapius is associated.

Some of the details of the chapter bear noting. First among these is the recognition, in the cult of Aesculapius, of the primacy of the claims of the flesh. On the grounds of the temple, set at a distance from it, are the Houses of Birth and Death, which mothers enter to give birth and old persons enter to die. Pater here strikes another blow for his theme of the continuity of life. The links between the living and the dead in "Change of Air" are more than a matter of pleasing landscape gardening. Another connection is the ageless quality of the members of the brotherhood; like nuns, or like Yeats's wild swans, or like the figures in the gold-decorated relief Marius gazed on, their ages are not readily apparent and their race continues even though an individual member may die. To Marius, his mind ever ready to be led by the author into quotation, "they appear eternally young, as many persons have seen them in many places—ministers and heralds of their father, passing to and fro over the earth, like gliding stars."[25]

The second striking thing about the chapter is the initiation of Marius into the rites of what might be called visual commitment. Not only does Marius come to admit the "morally salutary" influence of the "recognition of the beauty, even for the esthetic sense, of mere bodily health." He also admits the centrality of vision as his means of perceiving, indeed of loving. What Marius learns, through the tutelage of the young priest who comes to him in the night, is "a diligent promotion of the capacity of the eye, inasmuch as in the eye would lie for him the determining influence of life; he was of the number of those who, in the words of a poet who came long after, must be 'made perfect by the love of visible beauty.' "[26] The sanction of this belief is found by Marius in the *Phaedrus*. And in a remarkably subtle demonstration of the newly-expounded doctrine, Pater has Marius look from a hidden window in the shrine down a long landscape which leads certainly to Pisa and probably to Rome—a visual representation of Marius's future course in life. The life that is to come for Marius is a kind of painting: a new vista, seen as a whole and seen where no one would have thought such a vista possible.

"Change of Air" also suggests a kind of erotic initiation for Marius. Physical love seldom becomes overt in Pater, but throughout his writings one finds an intense preoccupation with male physical beauty. The suggestiveness of much of Pater makes some readers uneasy, but to ignore it or to pretend it does not exist would be an evasion of the obvious. The two forms of love which move Pater are maternal love (or its complement, filial love) and homosexual love. The former is apt to become in Pater a grandiloquent mythic idealization and the latter a kind of uneasy verbal-visual titillation. But both are potent forces and one must accept them as parts of Pater's emotional equipment which do not need so much to be psychoanalyzed as evaluated critically in the contexts in which they occur.

At "White-nights" Marius has been under the care

of his mother and has been fully dependent on her.
His father, indeed, is effectively removed from the scene,
so that the mother-son relationship is very much to the
fore. In "Change of Air" the appearance of the young
physician in the night has erotic overtones. Marius's
response is a combination of love and hero-worship.
"It would have been sweet to be the servant of him who
sat beside him speaking."[27] Marius recovers as much
from the tonic power of emotional allegiance as from
any medicinal remedy. After his experience at the
temple of Aesculapius, intense emotional attachment
comes easily to Marius, and in most cases the narrative
approves Marius's response.

Flavian, who succeeds the Aesculapian priest as
Marius's tutelary spirit, gains his power over Marius
largely from the visual impression he makes.[28] Unlike
Cornelius, Flavian never seems to be reticent or somehow removed from the reader's sympathy. His chief
characteristic, in spite of his literary ambitions, is his
splendid physical presence. And the impact of Flavian
remains with Marius. The degree to which Marius
accepts Cyrenaicism may be seen in Flavian's continuing
presence in the novel; Marius speaks of returning to
his friend's grave to weep, and Flavian's name recurs
at crucial moments, such as in the passage about the
divine companion. Marius's first attachment is a lasting
one, for the philosophy which Flavian represents is one
that Marius never abandons. The erotic element need
not be stressed very strongly, but it is present and it
colors Marius's philosophical allegiances, which come
to him, as to Goethe, "passionately, as in a person."

Marius's embracing of the Cyrenaic philosophy,
described in detail after the death of Flavian in "A
Pagan End," involves the casting off of the old religion.

There are no death throes; the religion of Numa has become "incredible" to Marius, and much as his attitudes are colored by it, he begins to put his trust in "the honest action of his own untroubled, unassisted intelligence."[29]

Marius's dedication, after the death of Flavian, to the free play of his own intelligence resembles the state of mind of the hero of *Gaston de Latour*. In the unfinished later work, which Pater intended as an extended Imaginary Portrait, Gaston, like Marius, must dispose of an old world of quasi-philosophical commitments for a new world of physical sensation. The continuity is less for Gaston than for Marius, however, for Marius has had his sensual perceptions heightened by his association with Flavian. But Gaston's movement from his medieval Christian background into the stream of experience, as described in a passage about Gaston's life at Chartres, is not unlike Marius's acceptance of Cyrenaicism:

> It was the brilliant surface with which the untried world confronted him. Touch it where you might, you felt the resistant force of the solid matter of human experience—of human experience, in its strange mixture of beauty and evil, its sorrow, its ill-assorted fates, its pathetic acquiescence; above all, in its over-powering certainty, over against his own world of echoes and shadows, which perhaps only seemed to be so much as echoes or shadows. A nature with the capacity of worship, he was straightway challenged, as by a rival new religion claiming to supersede the religion he knew, to identify himself conclusively with this so tangible world, its suppositions, its issues, its risks. Here was a world, certainly, which did not

halt in meditation, but prompted one to make
actual trial of it, with a liberty of heart which
likely enough traversed this or that precept (if it
were not rather a mere scruple) of his earlier con-
science. These its children, at all events, were, as
he felt, in instinctive sympathy with its motions;
had shrewd divinations of the things men really
valued, and waited on them with unquestioning
docility.[30]

Both Gaston and Marius feel a sense of reverence for
the panoramic life that confronts them, although
Marius's response is perhaps more meditative and
Gaston's more active.

One identifying feature of the old religion remains
for Marius in his new commitment to Cyrenaicism.
The linking of the abstract theory of commitment to
the physical particular (through the newly learned or
newly intensified power of vision) provides continuity,
since the religion of Marius's childhood was a religion
of places and things, of sense impressions, and since
Marius has learned the lesson of the sanctity of the
body at the temple of Aesculapius.

It was to the sentiment of the body, and the affections it defined—the flesh, of whose force and
colour that wandering Platonic soul was but so
frail a residue or abstract—he must cling. The
various pathetic traits of the beloved, suffering,
perished body of Flavian, so deeply pondered, had
made him a materialist, but with something of the
temper of a devotee.[31]

It is worth remembering that before he first sees Flavian,
Marius has already developed "an implicit epicurean-

ism," to which the sight of his new friend gives a physical sanction.[32]

Marius's enchantment with the physical form and particularly with the human form fits appropriately into the Cyrenaic scheme. The taste for metaphysics is no greater in the more mature Marius than it was in the young adherent to the old religion. From the commitment to physical form, the step is but a short one to the valuing of the moment.

> If he could but count upon the present, if a life brief at best could not certainly be shown to conduct one anywhere beyond itself, if men's highest curiosity was indeed so persistently baffled—then, with the Cyrenaics of all ages he would at least fill up the measure of that present with vivid sensations, and such intellectual apprehensions, as, in strength and directness and their immediately realized values at the bar of an actual experience, are most like sensations.[33]

Pater deals with the problem of public reaction to his position by noting the possible discriminations available to the Epicurean. Working from the kind of moral (even Victorian) Epicureanism outlined in William Wallace's treaties of 1880, Pater has the naturally temperate Aristippus exemplify the 'good' Cyrenaicism. The restatement in the ninth chapter of *Marius* of doctrines for which Pater had been attacked on their appearance in *The Renaissance* offers an opportunity for Pater to defend his dicta, and the chapter—Pater's part and the interpolations—is central to an understanding of the novel.

Pater notes that the Cyrenaic or Epicurean might interpret his delight as a moral delight: "My meat is

to do what is just and kind."[34] He notes that the soul—
a very Lockean soul which can apprehend nothing
beyond itself[35]—"never loses a sense of happiness in
conforming to the highest moral ideal it can clearly
define for itself."[36]

Certainly for Marius the commitment to Epicureanism is a moral one. His intention comprises what
Pater pointedly calls positive and negative qualities,
the negative being an effort to ascertain "the true limits
of man's capacities" and the positive being an effort to
achieve the "expansion and refinement of the power of
reception; of those powers, above all, which are immediately relative to fleeting phenomena, the powers
of emotion and sense."[37] This " 'aesthetic' education"
of Marius becomes equated with a movement towards
"whatever form of human life, in short, might be
heroic, impassioned, ideal."[38] Some of this ideality is
a quality of physical health; for those who had been
to the temple of Aesculapius, *salus* and salvation are
the same thing.[39] For Marius, the moral venture, with
the hazards Pater suggests (partly as a concession to his
critics), "would involve a life of industry, of industrious
study, only possible through healthy rule, keeping clear
the eye alike of body and soul."[40] Part of the delight
lies in the peril, and the test of success for Marius is
whether the choices he makes are the right ones. The
Epicurean's way of death which Marius chooses at the
end of the book allows Pater to have it both ways:
Marius puts his moral Cyrenaicism (Pater would have
pointed out that to link the terms would be redundant)
to work in dying a seemingly Christian death.

Stoicism, the second major philosophy which confronts Marius, appears dimly, as does the figure of
Marcus Aurelius, for Stoicism has no sensuous aspect

to which Pater can give us his impression. Marcus Aurelius never functions as a "divine companion" because Marius is never close enough to him. His disinterest puts him at one remove and makes him more a philosophical puzzle than a living example of deep commitment. Marcus Aurelius is remote, like a somewhat paternal personification of the state. In one sense he is the opposite of Marius; while Marius is curious about everything which confronts him, Marcus Aurelius is curious about nothing—or at least is curious only in the sense that he listens or asks questions; there is never any possibility, as there is with Marius, of commitment. Faustina, a more vivid figure, functions as a kind of reversal of Marius's mother. She fascinates the tender Marius because she is cruel, but her cruelty is a matter of titillation. Indeed, Marcus Aurelius's passivity draws more of Marius's contempt than Faustina's rumored vices, possibly because the emperor Marius sees does not conform to the idealistic preconception he has of him. One perceives Faustina clearly; seeing her through the eyes of Marius, the reader readily appreciates her intensely sensual impact. The battle between Cyrenaicism and Stoicism for the soul of Marius is never very open and the outcome is never very much in doubt. The former wins, largely because Marcus Aurelius, representing the highest development of Stoicism, bases his philosophy on anti-sensuous principles which contradict not only Cyrenaicism, but also the bases for Cyrenaicism, the religion of Numa and the dependence on visual perception as a means of apprehending truth.

At no point does Stoicism seem really very attractive to Marius. He comes close to admiring the emperor, but his admiration has reservations. Never do we sense that the Epicurean hero is about to cease his explorations of sensations and choose to ignore them, as Marcus Aurelius tries to do. For Marius, the Stoic's failing is his limitation of sympathies. Marcus Aurelius withdraws so far into himself that he cannot make the moral distinctions which have become part of the fabric of Marius's character. Thus when Marcus Aurelius, performing his public function of presiding over the gladiatorial combats, averts his eyes, attends to business, reads or seems otherwise indifferent, Marius judges him adversely:

> There was something in a tolerance such as this, in the bare fact that he could sit patiently through a scene like this, which seemed to Marius to mark Aurelius as his inferior now and for ever on the question of righteousness; to set them on opposite sides, in some great conflict, of which the difference was but a single presentment. . . . He [Marius] at least, the humble follower of the bodily eye, was aware of a crisis in life, in this brief, obscure existence, a fierce opposition of real good and real evil around him, the issues of which he must by no means compromise or confuse; of the antagonisms of which the "wise" Marcus Aurelius was unaware.[41]

Significantly, it is Marius's Cyrenaicism that keeps him from making Aurelius's moral error.

> His chosen philosophy had said,—Trust the eye: Strive to be right always in regard to the concrete experience: Beware of falsifying your impressions. And its sanction had at least been effective here in protesting—"This, and this, is what you may not look upon!"—Surely evil was a real thing,

> and the wise man wanting in the sense of it, where,
> not to have been, by instinctive election, on the
> right side, was to have failed in life.[42]

Marius's morality bases itself, of course, on instinctive sympathy rather than on principle, and his response to the gladiatorial combat is a triumph of intuition rather than dogma.

Marius sees in Stoicism's lack of concern for the physical the reason for its moral passivity or negation. Pater cites one point of "profound dissidence" between Marius and Marcus Aurelius. "The philosophic emperor was a despiser of the body."[43] Pater may well be criticizing the puritanical side of Victorian Christianity; the sensual emphasis is so consistent throughout his work that the same might be said of passages in the essays and in *Gaston de Latour*. Marius, whose Cyrenaicism and whose old religion insist equally on the physical point of reference for abstract thought, cannot approve of the emperor's withdrawal from the phenomena around him. In the arena, that withdrawal becomes a moral flaw, whereas Marius's commitment to physical sensation assumes morally positive magnitude in contrast. Again Pater's esthetic consistency and his public *apologia* coincide in *Marius*.

And as the court of Marcus Aurelius passes before us, Christianity enters the novel in the person of Cornelius, another Flavian, though ascetic and less interesting. Cornelius's physical presence exerts an influence on Marius; his body becomes a "sanction" of the "reverent delight" Marius takes in the human form, "the one true temple in the world."[44] About Marius's intense attachment to Cornelius, we can have no doubts. At the end, Marius chooses to have Cornelius go free as the one member of the party who is not a Christian, but "Marius believed that Cornelius was to be the husband of Cecilia; and that, perhaps strangely, had but added to the desire to get him away safely."[45] The public reading would be that Marius, having affection for Cecilia, does not want to see her married to Cornelius; the opposite, of course, is the case. Marius, being fond of Cornelius, does not want to see him married to Cecilia. The best Pater can have Marius feel for Cecilia is that she might make a good sister, although at one point he praises her "temperate beauty . . . [reminiscent] of the serious and virile character of the best female statuary of Greece."[46] Yet in spite of Marius's attachment to Cornelius, the latter is not the voluptuary Flavian is, and while he is a representation of the "divine companion," he is not a lover.

Marius's approach to Christianity is cautious, but Pater prepares the reader from the first page for the confrontation. In the face of Marcus Aurelius's Stoicism, Marius begins to long for a great experience which will give meaning to his life, the great confrontation of his Cyrenaic moral sensibility with the challenge of its own implications. He hopes to come to terms with those who live well in the world—that is, the early Christians.

> Where were those elect souls in whom the claim of Humanity became so amiable, so winning, persuasive—whose footsteps through the world were so beautiful in the actual order he saw—whose faces averted from him, would be more than he could bear? Where was that comely order to which as a great fact of experience he must give its due; to which, as to all other beautiful "phenomena" in life, he must, for his own peace, adjust himself?[47]

155

The Christianity Marius anticipates (and it is difficult to read the passage, for all its other implications, as anything less than an anticipation of the confrontation) makes its claim because of its "Humanity," because of its existence as "beautiful 'phenomena.' "

At every point Marius's Cyrenaicism prepares him for his Christian experiment. For example, his short experience of theism after the death of the emperor's son fits logically into his Epicureanism (it is another testing of what the world has to offer) and an anticipation of the Christianity that is still before him. Indeed, the theistic interlude exemplifies the Christian sensibility Marius develops before he learns anything of the Christian doctrine. Marius, for perhaps the only time in his passage through experience, senses a Creator in the material and presumably the spiritual world outside himself:

> Might not this entire material world, the very scene around him, the immemorial rocks, the firm marble, the olive-gardens, the falling water, be themselves but reflection in, or a cremation of, that one indefectible mind, wherein he too became conscious, for an hour, for a day, for so many years? . . . The purely material world, that close, impassable prison-wall, seemed just then the unreal thing, to be actually dissolving away all around him: and he felt a quiet hope, a quiet joy dawning faintly, in the dawning of his doctrine upon him as a really credible opinion.[48]

For Marius, however, the apprehension of a Creator in nature, while fitting nicely into his stream of experience, is a fleeting thing, not to recur. Yet as with any moral Epicurean, the contribution to the continuing experience makes the momentary vision, like all others, worthwhile, particularly because of its distinction and intensity:

> Himself—his sensations and ideas—never fell again precisely into focus as on that day, yet he was richer by its experience. But for once only to have come under the power of that peculiar mood, to have felt the train of reflections which belong to it really forcible and conclusive, to have been led by them to a conclusion, to have apprehended the *Great Ideal,* so palpably that it defined personal gratitude and the sense of a friendly hand laid upon him amid the shadows of the world, left this one particular hour a marked point in life never to be forgotten. . . . Must not all that remained of life be but a search for the equivalent of the Ideal, among so-called actual things—a gathering together of every trace or token of it, which his actual experience might present?[49]

Yet all this is anticipation.

Both the theistic experience and the Christian experiment to follow it are grounded in Marius's Epicureanism. They are in no sense an abandonment of his earlier philosophy, as some critics suggest, and the proof of this is in the chapter "Second Thoughts," which precedes the confrontation with a Creator in nature and which is devoted to a redefinition of the ideas expressed in "The New Cyrenaicism." In "Second Thoughts" we learn that Cyrenaicism "is ever the characteristic philosophy of youth, ardent, but narrow in its survey—sincere, but apt to become one-sided, or even fanatical. It is one of those subjective and partial ideals, based on vivid, because limited, apprehension of the truth of one aspect of experience."[50] Later on, Pater remarks that what such systems as Cyrenaicism need is "the complementary influence of some greater system, in which they may find their due place."[51] He goes on to note that the "ardent pre-occupation" with the fullness of experience is indeed valuable; that the Cyrenaic and the saint "would at least understand each other better than either would understand the mere man of the world."[52] At this point we may feel there is some justice in Eliot's charge that Pater and Arnold were attempting to replace religion with art. (The Cyrenaic who will be able to understand the saint is, significantly, "the Cyrenaic lover of beauty.") But with Pater, at least, the substitute is more than art.

The postulation of "a nobler form of Cyrenaicism" does not answer Pater's need of "some greater system." (The public was, of course, to read "greater system" to mean Christianity.) More nearly filling his requirements is the relativism which Marius finds in Rome, and of which the early church, unlike the later Christianity Pater to some extent disliked, partook. The "imperial system of organization" of which Marius finds himself a part—with all the "expanding power of a great experience"—is the relativistic synthesis which the capital city exemplifies and which is described in "Beata Urbs." In this "most religious city" a "blending of all the religions of the ancient world had been accomplished."[53] Yet for Marius, the city in which the body of Lucius Verus is consumed on its funeral pyre is a place very much full of human failings, and the higher synthesis is not in the civilization but in Marius's mind. What redeems Rome is indeed Marius's sympathetic acceptance of it as beautiful in all its frailty and all its variety. Aurelius's vision of the city is imperfect. Its faults are many; one of them is that it does not provide enough of "the light and beauty of the kingdom of nature, of

the natural man"—which it could have derived from
its pagan culture, from the Greek morality it had failed
to preserve—for the young Christian church to feed
upon, and the church therefore grows up somehow
alienated from the world as it loses its early freshness.
Marius in himself somehow comprises what the early
church, for all its pagan virtues, and Marcus Aurelius,
lack: a comprehensive sympathy and a power of conceiving of life as a whole. But the moment in which
he envisions this "greater system" of which his Cyrenaicism is part is the moment of his death. Marius's development of his sympathetic powers—so clearly evident
in his ultimate judgment on Marcus Aurelius—derives
from the rethinking of his Cyrenaicism. And the rethinking represents "not so much a change of practice,
as of sympathy—a new departure, an expansion, of
sympathy." As Pater notes at the very end of "Second
Thoughts," Marius's expansion of sympathy is but an
example of the consistency of his Epicurean philosophy.[54]

As Marius moves towards his confrontation with
Christianity, his expanded powers of sympathy make
him more receptive to a faith intensely felt by those
he loves. This power of sympathy combines with
another feature of Marius's character to make his acceptance of the rites which Cornelius and Cecilia
practice more understandable. Marius has a continuing
predilection for liturgical forms, and in the Christian
ritual he sees the forms he had practiced as a boy
re-created.

> The thirst for every kind of experience, en-
> couraged by a philosophy which taught that noth-
> ing was intrinsically great or small, good or evil,
> had ever been at strife in him with a hieratic

refinement, in which the boy-priest survived, prompting always the selection of what was perfect of its kind, with subsequent loyal adherence of his soul thereto. . . . in this strange family, like "a garden enclosed"—was the fulfillment of all the preferences, the judgments, of that half-understood friend [the mystic "companion"], which of late years had been his protection so often amid the perplexities of life.[55]

The "garden enclosed" reminds one of "The Child in the House" and confirms the impression that Christianity, in its early form, has for Marius much of the same appeal that his boyhood religion had.

Marius's Cyrenaic love of beauty also plays its part in securing his approbation of the religion of his new companions:

Worship—"the beauty of holiness," nay! the elegance of sanctity—was developed, with a bold and confident gladness, the like of which has hardly been the ideal of worship in any later age. The tables in fact were turned: the prize of a cheerful temper on a candid survey of life was no longer with the pagan world. The aesthetic charm of the Catholic Church, her evocative power over all that is eloquent and expressive in the better mind of man, her outward comeliness, her dignifying convictions about human nature:—all this, Dante and Giotto, by the great medieval church-builders, by the great ritualistists like Saint Gregory, and the masters of sacred music in the middle age—we may see already, in dim anticipation, in those charmed moments towards the end of the second century.[56]

The passage precedes Pater's great appreciation of the Roman Catholic liturgy, and certainly this is a part of the book where biographical criticism can be helpful. But the spirit of joy and repose that lies at the base of the liturgy, and the beauty with which that joy is reproduced esthetically, are the central points. Pater is evaluating his own response to liturgical forms and suggesting why they move him and what, at their best, they represent. The bases of the liturgy, as well as the forms themselves, secure Marius's emotional allegiance. The joy is, significantly, the same joy that had been found in Marius's rural home, the old pagan joy recaptured by the church in a chaotic world.

The early Renaissance of the church, as Pater calls it, is for Marius the distillation of all that is best in the pagan and Christian worlds: "the church was becoming 'humanistic.' "[57] One should recall Pater's definition in *The Renaissance* of humanism as a continuity of interest in whatever has once been the object of human sympathy. The Christian sacrifice, for example, recalls the sacrifice of Marius's boyhood; it is "a sacrifice, it might seem, like the most primitive, the most natural and enduringly significant of old pagan sacrifices, of the simplest fruits of the earth."[58] One recalls the family rites of the old religion, with their bread, oil, and wine, which anticipate the eucharistic celebration. Thus the sensuous appeal, through the forms of the liturgy, and the memorial appeal combine to win Marius's admiration for the new form of worship. And the new commitment, not conflicting with Marius's Epicureanism and not by any means complete or orthodox, prepares Marius for his sacrificial death. In one sense, Pater evades the issue of Christianity by having Marius die opportunely early. The impending conversion could hardly have been faced directly—given Pater's reluctance to commit himself absolutely to one philosophical system, unless it was Epicureanism—without defeating the purpose of the novel. As it is, Pater has his Christianity and avoids it, too.

The sacrificial death gains its sanctity not only because it identifies Marius as *"anima naturaliter Christiana,"* but also because it represents a reintegration of Marius's character. The Epicurean quest involves Marius in the flux, and the tension between his desire for rest and his desire to test his character against the sensations of the external world finds its resolution only in his death. For Marius, death comes as a last received, and to some extent willed, sensation. The extent to which the death is a Christian one need hardly trouble the reader, since the question has more to do with Pater's public purpose than with the consistency of *Marius.* U. C. Knoepflmacher, the most thorough and perceptive of recent critics of *Marius,* describes Marius's death effectively as "the Christian death of a pagan," noting that in Pater's scheme of things Christianity is "a strong possibility" for Marius but nothing more. Pater himself might have called it a "great possibility."[59] Knoepflmacher asserts that Marius's death is a parody of the myth of self-sacrifice "common to the religions of Christ and Apollo."[60] Quite so. But the death of Marius is sacrificial in the sense of being an act of religious commitment that destroys the self at the moment it makes the self whole.

To understand the full implications of Marius's death, it is necessary to understand the importance to the novel of the analogies between the old pagan religion and the religion of the young Christian church. The connections are made clear in the second chapter of *Marius,* "White-nights," the description of Marius's life at home with his mother.

The family home has its womblike characteristics.

Graham Hough notes that it takes no very subtle mind to interpret Pater's pre-Freudian "homesickness" in Freudian terms.[61] But the repose that the young Marius enjoys at White-nights, like Wordsworth's longed-for "repose that ever is the same," has sources separate from, if analogous to, the longing to return to the womb. White-nights and the religion practiced there and the similarity enclosed Christian community at the end of the book serve the esthetic purpose of providing a resolution of Marius's conflicting desires to be engaged in life and to attain a fixed philosophical position.

The argument of "White-nights," like that of much of Pater's writing, connects the reflective mind with the scene of repose, the setting being the implied cause of reflection; "to an instinctive seriousness, the material abode in which the childhood of Marius was passed had largely added."[62] Wright's plausible anecdote indicating Pater's belief in a Wordsworthian-Platonic preexistence may suggest a source for Marius's "instinctive seriousness," one of the non-Lockean features of his psychological makeup.[63] (Marius might be said to be born with two innate ideas: to accept the Lockean hypothesis about sense impressions and to carry it out to its full implications.) The main activity in White-nights is thinking: "surely nothing could happen there, without its full accompaniment of thought or reverie"; "you might . . . conceive . . . that dreaming even in the daytime might come to much there."[64] The "coy, retired place" retains its "picturesque charm" in spite of "workaday negligence." The negligence which makes White-nights charming results from the absence of any very active effort to keep the family estate up; its edenic qualities lie as much in the repose which requires little physical activity as in a pastoral realization of perfection. Significantly, the last member of Marius's family

to involve himself very much in the world about him—
"a certain Marcellus"—is a creature of history, having
lived two generations before. More important, however,
the picturesque charm links itself to the "elementary
conditions of life" which are to be so important to the
newly evolving Christian church. The influence of the
elemental conditions on the young Marius can hardly
be exaggerated, particularly since the resolution of the
novel relies on a subsuming of the fruits of the flux
into the elemental world of White-nights and the
Christian community. Pater's somewhat embarrassing
references to the warm fires and other attributes of a
pre-Kingsley Amis Merrie England reinforce the theme
of quiet in the midst of change, even if they seem
esthetically unsatisfactory.[65]

Mental activity in the midst of picturesqueness most
often takes the form of memory in Pater. Thus Marius's
mother lives with the memories of her dead husband,
who is a more real presence to her than to Marius:

> On the part of his mother . . . there was a sustained
> freshness of regret, together with the recognition,
> as Marius fancied, of some costly self-sacrifice to be
> credited to the dead. The life of the widow,
> languid and shadowy enough but for the poignancy
> of that regret, was like one long service to the de-
> parted soul; . . . To the dead, in fact, was conceded
> in such places a somewhat closer neighbourhood to
> the old homes they were thought still to protect . . .
> a closeness which the living welcomed, so diverse
> are the ways of our human sentiment.[66]

Marius's identification of maternal love as "the central
type of all love" results as much from the "protective-
ness" of his mother for all the selfhoods under her
care (Marius, his dead father, the wild birds of the

salt marsh which she forbids Marius to trap) as from an exclusive belief in the fulfillment of all his needs in her affection.

> Something pensive, spell-bound, and but half-real, something cloistral or monastic, as we should say, united to this exquisite order, made the whole place seem to Marius, as it were, *sacellum,* the peculiar sanctuary, of his mother, who, still, in real widowhood, provided the deceased Marius the elder with that secondary sort of life which we can give to the dead, in our intensely realised memory of them—the "subjective immortality," to use a modern phrase, for which many a Roman epitaph cries out plaintively to widow or sister or daughter, still in the land of the living. Certainly, if any such considerations regarding them do reach the shadowy people, he enjoyed that secondary existence, that warm place still left, in thought at least, beside the living, the desire for which is actually, in various forms, so great a motive with most of us.[67]

The memorial "chapel" of his mother indicates the sanctity of the closed circle where thought dominates, creates life by the power of the memory, and shows a "religious veneration for life as such."

Florian Deleal's sense of home is similar. In "The Child in the House" the working of the memory becomes the central mental activity:

> Tracing back the threads of his complex spiritual habit, as he was used in after years to do, Florian found that he owed to the place many tones of sentiment afterwards customary with him, certain inward lights under which things most naturally presented themselves to him. The coming and

going of travellers to the town along the way, the
shadow of the streets, the sudden breath of the
neighbouring gardens, the singular brightness of
bright weather there, its singular darknesses which
linked themselves in his mind to certain engraved
illustrations in the old big Bible at home, the
coolness of the dark, cavernous shops round the
great church, with its giddy winding stair up to
the pigeons and the bells—a citadel of peace in
the heart of trouble—all this acted on his childish
fancy, so that ever afterwards the like aspects and
incidents never failed to throw him into a well-
recognised imaginative mood, seeming actually
to have become a part of the texture of his mind.[68]

Memory sets the tone of Florian Deleal's mind, and his
moods, like those of Marius, depend on previous association—Pater had learned his lesson from Wordsworth well and Proust was to learn his from Pater.

Marius, like Florian, shows a moral "comeliness"
that depends on memory:

There would come, together with that precipitate
sinking of things into the past, a desire, after all,
to retain "what was so transitive." Could he but
arrest, for others also, certain clauses of experience,
as the imaginative memory presented them to himself! In those grand, hot summers, he would have
imprisoned the very perfume of the flowers. To
create, to live, perhaps, a little while beyond the
allotted hours, if it were but in a fragment of
perfect expression:—it was thus his longing defined itself for something to hold by amid the
"perpetual flux."[69]

The passage goes on to discuss how Marius conceives of
words as things. Barbara Charlesworth notes how

Pater endeavors to "hold the moment 'out of time,' " making "almost physical objects" of his memories.[70] So with Marius. We have seen how Pater works towards giving the reader a verbal artifact, the human form as a made thing, preserved in its fullness.[71] Like his mother's early "religious veneration for life as such,"[72] Marius's desire to capture the moments of his experience becomes the moral intention to preserve beauty; Marius's Epicureanism works for the preservation of the beautiful, which by Pater's definition includes the good.[73] Thus the need both for the flux, the time of cataloguing, and for the repose of White-nights and of the early church, the time of recall. Marius's final experience is the recalling of his whole life—an expanded version of emotion recollected in tranquillity.

Throughout the book Pater prepares us for Marius's final act of vision. The vision is anticipated when Marius first examines the implications of his new Cyrenaic philosophy after the death of Flavian:

> How will it look to me, at what shall I value it, this day next year?—that in any given day or month one's main concern was its impression for the memory. . . . Detached from him, yet very real, there lay certain spaces of his life, in delicate perspective, under a favourable light; and, somehow, all the less fortunate detail and circumstance had parted from them.[74]

And at the point where he has his experience of a Creator in nature, Marius has a dream which prefigures the moment of his death:

> In fact, the last bequest of this serene sleep had been a dream, in which, as once before, he overheard those he loved best pronouncing his name

very pleasantly, as they passed through the rich
light and shadow of a summer morning, along the
pavement of a city—Ah! fairer far than Rome![75]

While certainly a kind of Heavenly City, the city of
which Marius dreams is not particularly Christian since
most of those he has loved have little association with
Christianity. One of the functions of the divine companion, interestingly enough, is to help Marius preserve
his intense memories, which is a sufficient fact in itself
to prevent us from giving the companion a strictly
theological interpretation.

How had he longed, sometimes, that there were
indeed one to whose boundless power of memory
he could commit his own most fortunate moments,
his admiration, his love, Ay! the very sorrows of
which he could not quite bear to lose the sense:—
one strong to retain them even though he forgot,
in whose more vigorous consciousness they might
subsist for ever, beyond that mere quickening of
capacity which was all that remained of them for
himself! "Oh! that they might live before thee"
—To-day at least, in the peculiar clearness of one
privileged hour, he seemed to have apprehended
that in which the experiences he valued most
might find, one by one, an abiding place.[76]

In his theistic ruminations, Marius may be suggesting
that in the mind of God everything is lasting. Or he may
be suggesting that in his own intensity of vision, his
memories will be preserved—as is, indeed, the final
outcome. The highest vision of the dying Marius is
an act of memory, not a peculiarly Christian vision:

He would try to fix his mind, as it were im-
passively, and like a child thinking over the toys

it loves, one after another, that it may fall asleep thus, and forget all about them the sooner, on all the persons he had loved in life—on his love for them, dead or living, grateful for his love or not, rather than on theirs for him—letting their images pass again, or rest with him, as they would. In the bare sense of having loved he seemed to find, even amid the foundering of this ship that on which his soul might "assuredly rest and depend." One after another, he suffered those faces and voices to come and go, as in some mechanical exercise, as he might have repeated all the verses he knew by heart, or like the telling of beads one by one, with many a sleepy nod between-whiles.[77]

In dying, Marius exercises what Pater calls in "The Child in the House" "the finer sort of memory, bringing its object to mind with a great clearness, yet, as sometimes happens in dreams, raised a little above itself, and above ordinary retrospect."[78] This sanctifying memory gives to "the phenomena of experience a durability which does not really belong to them."[79] Thus Heraclitus's flux arrests itself in the moral memory —"a reduction to the abstract, of the brilliant road he travelled on, through the sunshine."[80] The arrested vision recalls Marius's childhood sense of "the whole of life . . . full of sacred presences, demanding of him a similar collectedness."[81]

The moment of death brings with it not only the fullness of sympathetic memory, but also a morally analogous identification with the rest of humanity; "the faces of these people [around Marius's bed], casually visible, took a strange hold on his affections; the link of general brotherhood, the feeling of human kinship, asserting itself most strongly when it was about to be severed for ever."[82] Most important of all, death brings Marius to the "great occasion of self-devotion . . . that should consecrate his life."[83] His death is, indeed, his highest act of moral passion.

> Revelation, vision, the discovery of a vision, the *seeing* of a perfect humanity, in a perfect world—through all his alternations of mind, by some dominant instinct, determined by the original necessities of his own nature and character, he had always set that above the *having,* or even the *doing,* of anything. . . . And how goodly had the vision been!—one last unfolding of beauty and energy in things, upon the closing of which he might utter his *"Vixi!"*[84]

Marius's vision has become the vision of the artist ordering his experience, particularly of the artist in the twentieth century. Diverse examples come to mind. There is Yeats's poem "Beautiful, Lovely Things," in which the poet provides verbal realizations of the faces of persons who have been important in his experience. There is Katharine Anne Porter's short story "The Jilting of Granny Wetherall," in which the dying woman finds satisfaction in her perception of the shades that gather round her bed. There is Federico Fellini's film *8 ½,* in which the confused protagonist finds fulfillment only when he confronts the sum total of his experience in the great dance at the conclusion. And there is Gabriel Conroy's less apocalyptic vision of Michael Furey in "The Dead." And Pater's own Duke Carl, who fully recognizes his selfhood only by undergoing two deaths, the first of which unites him in a sympathetic bond with both his people and the natural world and the second of which delivers him as an artifact of his moment in history to the humanists of later generations. The flux in each case turns into a repose in which only the mind is active and in which memory fuses the parts into a whole.

Marius in his death comes full circle. His vision of those he has loved concludes in the only way possible the path of a pensive person whose experience has been designed to sharpen the senses, to prepare for some larger seeing than the daily course of life could allow. The spiritual journey from White-nights to the Christian community gives Marius the materials for his vision. But he must reach a position of repose before the vision can be realized; the repose is, of course, death. Death comes as a more intense realization of the reflective days of his childhood; the novel comes full circle. Marius moves from thought through experience to more intense thought and simultantous resolution.

To a limited extent, one may take the whole narrative of Marius's life as the content of his final vision. The data of the flux are preserved. The fire of Heraclitus burns on, but the flame, arrested at its moment of perfection, becomes hard and gemlike. Restlessness and equilibrium, consumption and preservation—these unite in the final act of seeing. The acute perception of the visionary, which takes hard physical form, which becomes a mass of words, is something like "the form that Grecian goldsmiths make." Yeats's bird set upon a golden bough or his sages standing in the Heraclitean flames unconsumed exist as the visionary perceivers of the whole chain of experience—though experience, does not, in their transformed state, any longer affect them. They exist, like Marius, as latter-day adherents of the doctrine of the "Conclusion" to *The Renaissance;* like Marius in his vision, they are outside the flux, yet celebrate "what is past, or passing, or to come."

Notes

CHAPTER ONE

[1] W. B. Yeats, "Introduction," *The Oxford Book of Modern Verse* (New York, 1936), p. xxx.

[2] Yeats, "Introduction," p. xxx.

[3] Hereafter referred to as *Renaissance*. References, unless otherwise specified, are to the *New Library Edition of the Works of Walter Pater* (London, 1910). The edition is a corrected reprint of the 1900 Library Edition (London), with the addition of *Essays from 'The Guardian.'* The volumes cited hereafter are as follows:

1. *The Renaissance. Studies in Art and Poetry.*
2, 3. *Marius the Epicurean: His Sensations and Ideas* (cited as *Marius*, vols. 1, 2).
4. *Imaginary Portraits.*
5. *Appreciations; With an Essay on Style.*
6. *Plato and Platonism: A Series of Lectures.*
7. *Greek Studies: A Series of Essays.*
8. *Miscellaneous Studies: A Series of Essays.*
9. *Gaston de Latour: An Unfinished Romance.*
10. *Essays from 'The Guardian.'*

[4] "Preface," *Renaissance,* p. viii.

[5] "Preface," *Renaissance,* p. viii. Thomas Wright notes Pater's debt to Goethe's *Autobiography*. See Wright, *The Life of Walter Pater* (London, 1907), 1: 245.

[6] Kenneth Clark, "Introduction" to Pater, *The Renaissance* (Cleveland and New York, 1961), p. 25.

[7] "Wordsworth," *Appreciations,* p. 62.

[8] "Preface," *Renaissance,* p. viii.

[9] "Preface," *Renaissance,* p. x.

[10] "Preface," *Renaissance,* p. xi.

[11] "Preface," *Renaissance,* p. xiv. Clark notes that Pater "recognized more clearly than most professional historians of the nineteenth century the relationship of the Renaissance and the Middle Ages." Clark, "Introduction," pp. 14-15.

[12] "Preface," *Renaissance,* p. xiv.

Notes

13 In Yeats, *Essays and Introductions* (London, 1961), p. 472.

14 N. s., 29 (January 1866): 106-32. Part of the essay, entitled "Coleridge," was reprinted with additions in *Appreciations* (London, 1889). Citations are to "Coleridge's Writings" in *English Critical Essays (Nineteenth Century)*, ed. Edmund D. Jones (London, 1916), pp. 492-534. The essay does not appear in Pater's collected works.

15 "Coleridge's Writings," p. 493.

16 "Coleridge's Writings," p. 494.

17 "Coleridge's Writings," p. 534.

18 "Coleridge's Writings," p. 534. Pater does seem to use the terms modern and relativism interchangeably at times. His understanding of modernity, encouraged by theories of Darwin and others, seems to imply that in the 1800s the relativistic spirit had become the permanent historical condition. In his review of *A Century of Revolution* by W. S. Lilly (published in *The Nineteenth Century* 36 [December 1889]: 992-94), Pater asserts that after the eighteenth century, "There can be no lost causes." The modern, or relativist spirit, seemingly having become a permanent condition, would prevent the losses that had taken place before. See "A Century of Revolution," *Uncollected Essays* (Portland, Maine, 1903), pp. 117-18.

19 For the relationship between Darwin and Pater, see Philip Appleman, "Darwin, Pater, and a Crisis in Criticism," in *1859: Entering an Age of Crisis,* ed. Appleman and others (Bloomington, 1959), pp. 81-95.

20 T. S. Eliot, "Arnold and Pater," *Selected Essays,* new ed. (New York, 1950), especially pp. 436-38.

21 Eliot, "Arnold and Pater," p. 440.

22 Wright, *Life of Pater,* 1: 173-74.

23 Matthew Arnold, "Prefatory Note" to "On the Modern Element in Literature," in *On the Classical Tradition,* ed. R. H. Super (Ann Arbor, Michigan, 1960), p. 18.

24 Arnold, "Prefatory Note," p. 18.

25 Arnold, "Modern Element," pp. 21-22.

26 Arnold, "Modern Element," p. 32.

27 Arnold, "Modern Element," pp. 23-24.

28 Arnold, "Modern Element," p. 25.

29 "Coleridge's Writings," p. 493.

30 "Shadwell's Dante," *Uncollected Essays,* p. 156. The essay originally appeared as the "Introduction" to C. L. Shadwell's translation of *The Purgatory of Dante Alighieri* (London, 1892), pp. xiii-xxviii.

31 "Two Early French Stories," *Renaissance,* pp. 1-2.

Notes

32 "French Stories," p. 3.
33 "Symonds' 'Renaissance in Italy,'" *Uncollected Essays*, p. 7. Pater's review of a volume of J. A. Symonds's *The Renaissance in Italy: the Age of the Despots* appeared originally in *The Academy* 8 (31 July 1875) : 105-6.
34 "French Stories," pp. 6-7.
35 "French Stories," p. 24.
36 "French Stories," p. 26.
37 Wright, *Life of Pater*, 1: 226.
38 "French Stories," pp. 26-27.
39 "Botticelli," *Renaissance*, p. 55.
40 Eliot, "Arnold and Pater," pp. 440-41.
41 "Pico della Mirandola," *Renaissance*, pp. 48-49.
42 "Pico," p. 41.
43 "Pico," p. 46.
44 "Pico," p. 46.
45 "Pico," pp. 47-48.
46 Ezra Pound, *Guide to Kulchur* (London, 1938) , p. 160.
47 "Pico," p. 48.
48 The essay "Diaphaneitè" was printed postumously by Pater's literary executor, C. L. Shadwell, in *Miscellaneous Studies*, pp. 247-54.
49 "Diaphaneitè," p. 247.
50 "Diaphaneitè," p. 247.
51 Wright, *Life of Pater*, 1: 216-17.
52 "Diaphaneitè," p. 248.
53 "Diaphaneitè," p. 248.
54 "Diaphaneitè," pp. 248-49.
55 "Diaphaneitè," p. 249.
56 Reprinted with permission of The Macmillan Company from *Collected Poems* by William Butler Yeats. Copyright 1924 by The Macmillan Company, renewed 1952 by Bertha Georgie Yeats.
57 Pp. 24-27.
58 The projected "self-delighting" of the daughter reminds us of the young Marius looking forward to his "great occasion of self-devotion." See *Marius the Epicurean*, 1: 18.
59 "Diaphaneitè," p. 250.
60 Reprinted with permission of The Macmillan Company from *Collected Poems* by William Butler Yeats. Copyright 1933 by The Macmillan Company, renewed 1961 by Bertha Georgie Yeats.
61 "The Poetry of Michelangelo," *Renaissance*, pp. 96-97.
62 "Michaelangelo," p. 97.
63 "The School of Giorgione," *Renaissance*, p. 135.
64 "School of Giorgione," p. 135.

Notes

[65] "School of Giorgione," pp. 130-31.

[66] "School of Giorgione," pp. 133-34.

[67] "School of Giorgione," pp. 137-38.

[68] "School of Giorgione," p. 140.

[69] J. A. Crowe and G. B. Cavalcaselle in *A History of Painting in North Italy* (London, 1870) set about revising the Giorgione *oeuvre* drastically. Kenneth Clark comments in a note in his edition of *The Renaissance* (p. 136) that the judgments of Crowe and Cavalcaselle on Giorgione were largely erroneous.

[70] Pater laments that we know the late date of Botticelli's death because the knowledge allows so much unhappy speculation about Botticelli's declining years. (See "Botticelli," p. 51.) Fortunately, Giorgione's scant history permits happier speculations.

[71] "School of Giorgione," p. 148.

[72] "School of Giorgione," p. 151.

[73] "Conclusion," *Renaissance,* p. 233.

[74] "Winckelmann," *Renaissance,* p. 231.

[75] "Conclusion," p. 236.

[76] "Diaphaneitè," p. 250.

[77] "Pico," p. 46.

CHAPTER TWO

[1] "Aesthetic Poetry," *Appreciations,* first ed. (London, 1889), pp. 216-17.

[2] "Aesthetic Poetry," p. 217.

[3] "Postscript," *Appreciations* (Library Edition, 1910), pp. 241-61. All subsequent references are to this edition.

[4] "Postscript," pp. 245-46.

[5] "Postscript," p. 246.

[6] Bayley, *The Romantic Survival* (London, 1957), p. 45.

[7] "Postscript," p. 241.

[8] "Dante Gabriel Rossetti," *Appreciations,* p. 212.

[9] "Wordsworth," *Appreciations,* pp. 60-61.

[10] "Postscript," pp. 258-59.

[11] "Postscript," p. 259.

[12] "Postscript," pp. 241-42.

[13] "Botticelli," *Renaissance,* p. 52.

[14] "Botticelli," pp. 52-53.

[15] John Ruskin wrote in 1874 of the linear qualities of Botticelli's work. See "The Schools of Florence," *Val d'Arno* (London,

176

Notes

1874). See also *The Works of John Ruskin,* ed. E. T. Cook and Alexander Wedderburn 23 (London, 1906) : 265-66.

16 Pater's analysis of Botticelli was quickly assimilated by his contemporaries. Symonds, in the third volume of *The Renaissance in Italy* (London, 1877), states: "For us . . . [Botticelli] has an almost unique value as representing the interminglement of antique and modern fancy at a moment of transition" (p. 250). At another point, Symonds disagrees specifically with Pater's interpretation of "The Coronation of the Virgin" in the Uffizi, but the disagreement merely confirms the strong impression Pater's criticism had made in the decade after its first appearance (n. 2, pp. 254-55). Considering Symonds's opinion of Pater, any acknowledgment of indebtedness, if such would have been appropriate or necessary, was unlikely. See Phyllis Grosskurth, *John Addington Symonds: A Biography* (London, 1964), especially pp. 157-58. See also Bernard Berenson, *The Passionate Sightseer* (London, 1960), pp. 176-77, and *Sunset and Twilight,* ed. Nicky Mariano (London, 1966), pp. 23, 343.

17 See especially René Wellek, *A History of Modern Criticism: 1750-1950. The Later Nineteenth Century* (London, 1966), pp. 381-83.

18 "Leonardo da Vinci," *Renaissance,* pp. 124-26.

19 Kenneth Clark, *Leonardo da Vinci,* second ed. (Cambridge, 1962), p. 117.

20 "The School of Giorgione," *Renaissance,* pp. 151-52.

21 "Joachim du Bellay," *Renaissance,* p. 176.

22 "Conclusion," *Renaissance,* p. 235.

23 "Raphael," *Miscellaneous Studies,* p. 39.

24 "Postscript," p. 256.

25 Pater almost certainly had not read Burckhardt before 1878, the date of the Middlemoor translation. Burckhardt's book had only a small circulation, even in Switzerland and Germany, in the early 1870s. See Jacob Burckhardt, *The Civilisation of the Renaissance in Italy,* 3d rev. ed. (London, 1950), p. 81.

26 "Winckelmann," *Renaissance,* p. 201.

27 "Two Early French Stories," *Renaissance,* p. 15.

28 "The Poetry of Michelangelo," *Renaissance,* p. 73.

29 "Michaelangelo," p. 75.

30 "Winckelmann," p. 206.

31 "Winckelmann," p. 205.

32 "Pico della Mirandola," *Renaissance,* p. 49.

33 "Winckelmann," p. 182.

34 "Winckelmann," p. 224.

35 "Winckelmann," pp. 213-14.

Notes

36 "Winckelmann," pp. 229-30.
37 "Wordsworth," pp. 62-63.
38 "Wordsworth," p. 54.
39 "Winckelmann," p. 228.

CHAPTER THREE

1 Richard Ellmann, "The Backgrounds of 'The Dead,'" *James Joyce* (New York, 1959), pp. 252-63.

2 James Joyce, "The Dead," *Dubliners* (London, 1914), pp. 277-78.

3 R. V. Johnson, *Walter Pater: A Study of His Critical Outlook and Achievement* (Melbourne, 1961), pp. v-vi. Johnson discusses the attacks on Pater's impressionism.

4 "Winckelmann," *Renaissance,* pp. 221-22.

5 Particularly important in this regard are four chapters (lectures) of *Plato and Platonism:* "Plato and the Doctrine of Motion," "The Genius of Plato," "The Republic," and "Plato's Aesthetics."

6 "Genius of Plato," p. 129.

7 Among the visual arts one might well include drama. In his essay on *Measure for Measure* in *Appreciations* (p. 180), Pater's description of Claudio as a "flowerlike young man" exemplifies his visual emphasis. He describes the play, characteristically enough, as "the new body of a higher, though sometimes remote and difficult poetry, escaping from the imperfect relics of the old story" and as having "a profoundly designed beauty" (p. 173). The human analogy, particularly as linked with beauty, anticipates Pater's assertion that Plato makes each dialogue "like a single living person" ("Genius of Plato," p. 129).

8 "Genius of Plato," pp. 135-35.

9 *Pater's Portraits: Mythic Pattern in the Fiction of Walter Pater* (Baltimore, 1967), p. 99.

10 "Winckelmann," pp. 205-6.

11 Wright, *The Life of Walter Pater* (London, 1907), 1: 216.

12 Wright, *Life of Pater,* 1: 193.

13 "Wordsworth," *Appreciations,* p. 62.

14 Arthur Symons, "Introduction," *The Renaissance* (Modern Library edition, New York, n.d.), p. xiii.

15 *Marius the Epicurean,* 1: 49-50.

16 "An English Poet," in *Imaginary Portraits. A New Collec-*

178

tion, ed. Eugene J. Brzenk (New York, 1964), pp. 47, 49. The fragment first appeared in *The Fortnightly Review* (1 April 1931).

[17] "Winckelmann," p. 207.

[18] "Emerald Uthwart," *Miscellaneous Studies,* pp. 220-21.

[19] Graham Hough's treatment of Pater's eroticism is particularly succinct and to the point. Yet one wonders whether "the half-fear of sensuous impressions" is so prevalent as Hough believes. Perhaps the half-fear is of having the sensuous impressions interpreted correctly. Hough's analysis of the pictorial sensibility in Pater's writings tangentially supports the theory of the human form as artifact. The full implications of Hough's masterful chapter on Pater in *The Last Romantics* (London, 1949) have yet to be worked out.

[20] "The Age of Athletic Prizemen," *Greek Studies,* pp. 269-99.

[21] See especially Hough, *Last Romantics,* p. 163.

[22] Hough, *Last Romantics,* p. 163.

[23] "Athletic Prizemen," pp. 274-75.

[24] "Athletic Prizemen," p. 276.

[25] "Emerald Uthwart," pp. 245-46.

[26] "Athletic Prizemen," p. 282.

[27] "Athletic Prizemen," p. 284.

[28] "Athletic Prizemen," pp. 297-98.

[29] "Winckelmann," p. 217.

[30] "Duke Carl of Rosenmold," *Imaginary Portraits,* pp. 119-53.

[31] "Duke Carl," p. 153.

[32] "Aesthetic Poetry," *Sketches and Reviews,* ed. Albert Mordell (New York, 1919), p. 19.

[33] *Marius,* 1: 119.

[34] *Marius,* 2: 204-5.

[35] *Marius,* 2: 207.

[36] *Marius,* 2: 138-39.

[37] "Athletic Prizemen," p. 299.

[38] "Pico della Mirandola," *Renaissance,* p. 49.

CHAPTER FOUR

[1] "Style," *Appreciations,* pp. 11-12.

[2] Edmund Chandler, "Pater on Style," *Anglistica* 11 (1958): 100.

[3] See Philip Appleman, "Darwin, Pater, and a Crisis in Crit-

icism," in *1859: Entering An Age of Crisis,* ed. Appleman and others (Bloomington, 1959), pp. 81-95.

⁴ R. T. Lenaghan discusses the Hegelian elements in Pater as a continuing repetition of thesis and antithesis. See his "Pattern in Pater's Fiction," *Studies in Philology* 58 (January 1961): 69-91. See also Bernard Behr, "Pater and Hegel," *Englische Studien* 50 (1916-1917): 300-308.

⁵ Pp. 233-39.

⁶ "Denys L'Auxerrois," *Imaginary Portraits,* p. 47.

⁷ "Denys," p. 48.

⁸ "Denys," p. 51.

⁹ "Denys," pp. 62-63.

¹⁰ "Denys," pp. 53-54.

¹¹ "Denys," p. 55-56.

¹² "Denys," p. 56.

¹³ "Denys," p. 58.

¹⁴ "Denys," p. 58.

¹⁵ "A Study of Dionysus," *Greek Studies,* pp. 9-52.

¹⁶ "Dionysus," pp. 9-10.

¹⁷ "Dionysus," p. 10.

¹⁸ "Sir Thomas Browne," *Appreciations,* pp. 152-53.

¹⁹ "Postscript," *Appreciations,* p. 242.

²⁰ Yeats employs the tapestry image frequently in his early poetry in ways similar to Pater's.

²¹ "Denys," p. 60.

²² "Denys," p. 61.

²³ "Denys," p. 71.

²⁴ See Lenaghan, "Pattern in Pater's Fiction," for a lengthy discussion of the opposition between the two; U. C. Knoepflmacher calls the Appolonian and Dionysiac forces rest and motion respectively. See Knoepflmacher, *Religious Humanism and the Victorian Novel* (Princeton, 1965), pp. 165-67.

²⁵ "Denys," pp. 75-76.

²⁶ One might be justified in reading the new lord of Auxerre as a symbol of either Apollonian paganism or Christianity. The former might be argued because the new lord virtually ignores the music of Denys's organ; but Pater makes very little of the fact. The latter seems more likely. In the country of the vine, however, Dionysiac figures will continue to reappear, and the important point is that the complexity of Auxerre continues to center around the human form and the cathedral.

²⁷ "Winckelmann," *Renaissance,* pp. 186-88.

²⁸ *Gaston de Latour,* pp. 36-38.

²⁹ In his review of J. A. Symonds's *The Italian Renaissance* see

Notes

(*Uncollected Essays,* pp. 11-12), Pater rebukes the author's lack of reserve and discretion. The reticent Pater doubtless delighted in the care with which his cathedral boys hide their dice.

30 "Two Early French Stories," *Renaissance,* p. 26.

31 *Gaston de Latour,* p. 30.

32 "Notre-Dame d'Amiens," *Miscellaneous Studies,* pp. 109-10.

33 "Notre-Dame d'Amiens," pp. 119-20.

34 "Vézelay," *Miscellaneous Studies,* p. 135.

35 "Vézelay," p. 141.

CHAPTER FIVE

1 *Marius the Epicurean,* 2: 67.

2 *Marius,* 2: 70.

3 See especially Helen H. Young, *The Writings of Walter Pater: A Reflection of British Philosophical Opinion from 1860 to 1890* (Lancaster, Pennsylvania, 1933).

4 5 April 1885, quoted in Horatio F. Brown, *John Addington Symonds, A Biography* (London, 1895), 2: 246. Phyllis Grosskurth, Symonds's recent biographer, succinctly contrasts Symonds with Pater, noting that Symonds, with his breadth of interests and involvement in life, is the more typically Victorian. The largeness of his literary output likewise argues the point. Some of Symonds's poorly concealed contempt for Pater results from what he doubtless felt to be the complementary preciosity of Pater's life and writings. Pater's retiring social life and his suggestive, rather than explicit, prose would have bothered Symonds, who thought of himself as a more frank writer and *homme engagé.* See Grosskurth, *John Addington Symonds: A Biography* (London, 1964), p. 224 n.

5 See especially the following evaluations of *Marius:* Graham Hough, *The Last Romantics* (London, 1949), John Pick, "Divergent Disciples of Walter Pater," *Thought* 23 (March 1948): 114-28; R. V. Osbourn, *"Marius the Epicurean,"* *Essays in Criticism,* n.s., 1 (1951): 387-403; C. M. Bowra, "Walter Pater," in *Inspiration and Poetry* (London, 1955), pp. 199-219; Iain Fletcher, *Walter Pater,* Writers and Their Works, no. 114 (London, 1959), pp. 23-28; Bernard Duffey, "The Religion of Pater's *Marius,"* *Texas Studies of Literature and Language* 2 (Spring 1960): 103-14; Germain d'Hangest, "La genese de 'Marius l'Epicurien' " and "Marius l'Epicurien," in *Walter Pater: L'homme et l'oeuvre*

Notes

(Paris, 1961), pp. 270-337; Billie Andrew Inman, "The Organic Structure of *Marius the Epicurean*," *Philological Quarterly* 41 (April 1962): 475-91; Louise M. Rosenblatt, "The Genesis of *Marius the Epicurean*," *Comparative Literature* 14 (Summer 1962): 242-60; and U. C. Knoepflmacher, "The 'Atmospheres' of *Marius the Epicurean*," in *Religious Humanism and the Victorian Novel* (Princeton, 1965), pp. 189-233.

6 William Sharp, *Papers Critical and Reminiscent* ([London], 1912), p. 212. Sharp gives the date as 1883, but 1884 may in fact be more accurate.

7 Among the former are Thomas Wright, Sharp, and, most recently, Inman; Fletcher and Knoepflmacher are among the latter.

8 See Wright's account of Pater's support of the Christian emphasis in *Marius (The Life of Walter Pater* [London, 1907], 1:86-88). Pater had praised William Sharp's review of *Marius* in *The Athenaeum* (28 February 1885, pp. 271-73), which noted the Christian element.

9 See above chapter 1, pp. 8-20.

10 "Pater, Mr. Rose, and the 'Conclusion' of *The Renaissance*," *Essays and Studies* 32 (1946): 44-60.

11 W. H. Mallock, *The New Republic* (London, 1877), 2: 19.

12 J. H. Buckley, "Pater and the Suppressed Conclusion," *Modern Language Notes* 65 (April 1950): 249-51.

13 Pater admits as much in the footnote to the slightly revised "Conclusion" in the third edition of *The Renaissance* (London, 1888), p. 233. Although Thomas Wright argues that Mallock's satire did not affect Pater seriously, indeed that Pater enjoyed being the object of attention, A. C. Benson, among others, holds the opposite opinion. Wright gives little documentation for his assertion. Benson, on this issue, has the more solid support of later scholarship, specially of Tillotson and Buckley. See Wright, *Life of Pater,* 2: 17-18; and Benson, *Walter Pater* (London, 1966), pp. 52-54.

14 "The Doctrine of Plato," *Plato and Plantonism,* p. 178.

15 "The Republic," *Plato and Platonism,* p. 240.

16 Pater interpolates several adapted passages, notably the Cupid and Psyche tale from Apuleius, the aphorisms of Marcus Aurelius, and the conversation between Lucian and Hermotimus. The passages give a suggestion of authenticity to the historical setting of the novel, as well as serving specific purposes in the development of the narrative.

17 *Marius,* 1: 3.

18 *Marius,* 1: 3-4.

Notes

19 *Marius*, 1: 4.

20 Wright, *Life of Pater*, 2: 31-42.

21 *Marius*, 1: 5.

22 Mrs. Humphrey Ward, review of *Marius, Macmillan's Magazine* 52 (May 1885) : 132-38.

23 "The Child in the House," *Miscellaneous Studies*, pp. 180-81.

24 "Child in the House," p. 176.

25 *Marius*, 1: 38.

26 *Marius*, 1: 32.

27 *Marius*, 1: 31.

28 *Marius*, 1: 49-50.

29 *Marius*, 1: 125.

30 *Gaston de Latour*, p. 38.

31 *Marius*, 1: 125.

32 *Marius*, 1: 46.

33 *Marius*, 1: 144.

34 *Marius*, 1: 145.

35 For a discussion of the Lockean assumptions implicit in Pater's work, see Ernest Lee Tuveson, *The Imagination as a Means of Grace* (Berkeley, 1960), pp. 87-88.

36 *Marius*, 1: 145.

37 *Marius*, 1: 147.

38 *Marius*, 1: 152.

39 *Marius*, 1: 28.

40 *Marius*, 1: 156.

41 *Marius*, 1: 241-42.

42 *Marius*, 1: 243.

43 *Marius*, 2: 53.

44 *Marius*, 2: 53-54.

45 *Marius*, 2: 212.

46 *Marius*, 2: 105.

47 *Marius*, 2: 12.

48 *Marius*, 2: 69-70.

49 *Marius*, 2: 71-72.

50 *Marius*, 2: 15.

51 *Marius*, 2: 19.

52 *Marius*, 2: 20.

53 *Marius*, 1: 184.

54 *Marius*, 2: 27-28.

55 *Marius*, 2: 107.

56 *Marius*, 2: 123.

57 *Marius*, 2: 95-96, 125.

58 *Marius*, 2: 136.

59 Knoepflmacher, *Religious Humanism*, pp. 219-21.

[60] Knoepflmacher, *Religious Humanism,* p. 221.

[61] *Last Romantics,* pp. 166-67.

[62] *Marius,* 1: 13.

[63] Wright, *Life of Pater,* 2: 62. Wright asserts that Pater told Richard C. Jackson of men being "born out of due season" and remarking, "Pansies are the eyes of the angels, given to mankind so that they should not weep."

[64] *Marius,* 1: 13-14.

[65] In connection with the parallelism between White-nights and Pater's England, it is worthwhile to cite Hough's identification of Marius's childhood religion of Numa with Pater's childhood Angelicanism. See Hough, *Last Romantics,* pp. 148-49.

[66] *Marius,* 1: 17.

[67] *Marius,* 1: 20-21.

[68] "Child in the House," pp. 175-76.

[69] *Marius,* 1: 154-55.

[70] *Dark Passages* (Madison and Milwaukee, 1965), p. 42.

[71] See chapter 3 above.

[72] *Marius,* 1: 27.

[73] See especially *Marius,* 1: 144-46.

[74] *Marius,* 1: 154.

[75] *Marius,* 2: 62-63.

[76] *Marius,* 2: 70-71.

[77] *Marius,* 2: 222-23.

[78] "Child in the House," p. 171.

[79] *Marius,* 1: 129.

[80] *Marius,* 1: 165.

[81] *Marius,* 1: 17.

[82] *Marius,* 2: 217.

[83] *Marius,* 1: 18.

[84] *Marius,* 2: 218.

Index

This book has been set in Linotype Baskerville
with Bulmer & Castellar display and printed
by the Printing Department of the
University of Kentucky. Design
by Jonathan Greene.